This book may be ordered by e-mail at: John@BodySpiritSoul77.com or
By Website at: www.BodySpiritSoul77.com

Because of the dynamic nature of the Internet, any web addresses or links contained in this book may have changed since publication and may no longer be valid. The views expressed in this work are solely those of the author.

The author of this book does not dispense medical advice or prescribe the use of any technique as a form of treatment for physical, emotional or medical problems without the advice of a physician, either directly or indirectly. The intent of the author is only to offer information of a general nature to help his readers in their quest for emotional and spiritual well-being. In the event the reader(s) use any of the information contained in this book for themselves, which is their constitutional right, the author (and publisher) assume no responsibility for the reader(s) actions or outcome.

FIRST PRINTING: JUNE 2016

SECOND PRINTING: October 2016

I would like to thank all of my friends that helped me while I wrote this series of books. To all my friends – Jean, Tom, Ashley, Linda, Bridget, and everyone else that supported me, Thank You.

Also, in fond memory of my best friend my Golden Retriever Wind Runner.

THE CODE

The code is quite simple: it is a philosophy of life that explains the emotional and spiritual healing event that is life. The prophecy, "The Revelations of Christ" is the key to understanding the entire Bible in context.

The parables of the New Testament explain the healing process for both people individually and mankind collectively. This healing is something that happens naturally through creation and evolution.

The book of Genesis explains the first scene of the prophecy which is the beginning of creation itself and the evolution of creation that continued from that point in time until today.

Exodus and the Old Testament are the second scene of the prophecy and the second time in the evolution of the collective spirit of mankind.

The New Testament is the third scene of the prophecy and the beginning of the third time of mankind's evolution through creation.

The Bible's code is quite simple there are two events described in each time
  1) A significant spiritual event –
      a. The first three chapter of the book of Genesis (Creation)
      b. Moses demonstrating unconditional love for the Israelites (Exodus)
      c. Jesus planting the seeds of love and forgiveness in the collective spirit of mankind (The New Testament's books of Matthew, Mark, Luke and John).
  2) The chronicling of the experiences of mankind that followed the significant spiritual event. The purpose for chronicling our experiences is to know the impact of each significant spiritual event on the collective spirit and soul of mankind.
      a. Chapters 4 – 50 of the book of Genesis
      b. The Old Testament
      c. The history of mankind's evolution after the time of Jesus has not been completed

Since the New Testament only contains the significant spiritual event it is not complete and the history of this time in the evolution of mankind must be written.

The healing event the parables of the New Testament explain the healing of a broken spirit; it is the healing of the mind. The psychology of the parables takes Jungian psychology to a much deeper level.

The Bible and its stories integrate a philosophy of life into the psychology needed to heal the broken spirit that exists in many people individually and all of mankind collectively. The healing of the mind is the healing of the collective spirit of mankind. The end of time that many people refer to is about the completion of the events that will integrate all the individual spirits of mankind into one body, one spirit and one soul – one being of love and light one being of pure consciousness. It is about the healing of Adam, the first being that was the first spirit and soul; the first broken spirit.

TABLE OF CONTENTS

CHAPTER 1 – IN THE BEGINNING

1) In the beginning there was Adam (a complete being in spirit and soul was created) and then there was Adam and eve (the first broken spirit).
2) In the beginning god created creation then the lord god let the spirit of that which was created evolve.
3) The history of mankind's understanding of gods and God.

CHAPTER 2 – THE BROKEN SPIRIT

1) The son of man
2) The son of man walking among 7 candlesticks
3) The 7 churches
4) The mystery of the seven stars, 7 angels, seven candlesticks and 7 churches
5) The seven churches

CHAPTER 3 – GOD'S PLAN TO HEAL ALL OF MANKIND   71

THE LAMB AND THE BOOK WITH SEVEN SEALS

THEN THERE WAS MAN (ADAM AND EVE ARE NOW CLOTHED IN SKIN)

1) The lamb (the evolution of mankind)
2) The book with 7 seals (the book of the knowledge of dark and light)
3) The 12 tribes of 12,000 members per tribe that are the 144,000 that are sealed
4) The 7 angels with 7 trumpets
5) The mystery of the angel with the little book that tastes sweet but turns bitter

CHAPTER 4 – PHASE TWO OF THE PLAN   100

THE WOMAN ABOUT TO GIVE BIRTH TO A CHILD AND A DRAGON WITH SEVEN HEADS WAITING TO CONSUME THE CHILD

MANKIND'S EVOLUTION FROM THE TIME OF JESUS

1) The woman about to five birth to a child
2) A dragon waiting to consume the child (has 7 heads and 10 horns)
3) A beast that rises up from the sea with similar characteristics as the dragon
4) A beast that comes from the earth (looks like a lamb and has 2 horns)
5) The lamb and the 144,000 and the great winepress
6) The mystery of Babylon

AUTHORS COMMENT

There have been many people that researched the meaning of the images and symbols of this age old prophecy. Most of these interpretations had a negative and destructive explanation of the prophecy. These interpretations said that God was going to destroy all of mankind by sending its demons into the world. As you read this book you will learn that these older interpretations were true but were only true as it relates to a darker collective spirit and the reality mankind created because our collective spirit was not as light as it is today. Today many people have evolved spiritually and are challenging these older, darker interpretations. As we evolve spiritually we are learning to leave these older interpretations behind. This is because as we evolve the spirit of mankind which is God evolves and this results in a new spirit of the prophecy.

For many years I listened to many people from many faiths tell me what was right and wrong with the world from the perspective of their beliefs. They also shared with me their understanding of God and Creation and many shared their perspective on the writings of the Bible and the prophecy "The Revelations of Christ".

As time went on I felt there was something amiss with what everyone told me. It was as if a lot of what I was being told was the same thing just from a slightly different perspective. One day I started reading the prophecy Revelations. As I read it I wanted to unravel its truths no matter what they would be. I was committed to learning the truth behind its images and symbols. As time went on I continued to read it. I read it from front to back and even back to front. Sometimes I even started reading it in the middle and then read it to the end and then went back to the middle and read it backwards. I read it for more than 10 years. Then one day I started to listen to the spirit of the prophecy and the spirit of the parables and the spirit of the book of Genesis and wrote what it had to share with me.

What I learned is contained in this book.

The original authors of the Bible had a great challenge in front of them. They had to present to the leaders of the Roman Empire with a book that contained all the spiritual beliefs of the tribes and nations of those that were ruled by the Romans. There was one truth that Rome's leaders would not allow them to have in this book. It was the truths about creation and our ability to create through our body, spirit and soul. These Roman leaders were using their knowledge of creation and how it works to use the collective spirit of their empire to manage their empire. The four horsemen of Revelations define the four pillars of their strategy. One of the most important results of the Roman Empire's strategy to manage its territory was the suppression of the spirit of those under its rule. The original authors of the Bible hid these truths about creation along with the truths about the body, spirit and soul in the images and symbols of the prophecy, "The Revelation of Christ", the parables of the New Testament and the book of Genesis. These truths are also hidden in many of the prayers and rituals of traditional religions.

The original authors of the Bible (and the documents that became the Bible) chronicled the history of the lives of the families and tribes in the Middle East through the story of the family of Israel. The Israelites history included the interactions of all the nations of the Middle East; so it was the best story to use to tell the story of how the collective spirit of the Israelites manifested in the Israelite's lives. They preserved the knowledge of the body, spirit and soul and its evolution through creation in the prophecy, "The Revelations of Christ" and the parables of Jesus. The prophecy tells the story of the collective spirit's journey into a darker reality and then the eventual evolution into what it refers to as the New Holy City of Jerusalem. The prophecy tells the story of mankind's spiritual evolution into a dark reality through three scenes. These three scenes are the first three times in the evolution of creation. Many people talk about the end of time. There are many phases in the evolution of the spirit of man. Each of these phases is a time. The end of each phase is the end of a time. The prophecy describes these times as:

1) The beginning of time – The Son of Man walking among seven candlesticks and the seven churches with and angel in each church.

2) The beginning of mankind's potential to create light – The plan of Moses. Moses lived with unconditional love for the Israelites and released the seals that sealed the book of knowledge of love and light away from mankind's consciousness. This released a greater power of creation into the life of the Israelites.

   a. The seven angels with seven trumpets chronicle the time between the death of Moses and the time that Jesus came to save our collective spirits and souls.

3) The new plan to use future generations of children to bring a greater light into the world to aid in the process of creating light. The prophecy explains this new plan through the images and symbols of a woman about to give birth to a child, a dragon waiting to consume the child and two beasts. There are also seven angels filled with plagues that are holding cups that define the unhealthy state of spirit that existed at the time when Jesus lived with us.

   a. Post Jesus until today as mankind has struggled to learn to forgive and live with love while transforming the spirit of their creations during a time when we lived with a collective spirit not capable of holding light; which the prophecy refers to as Babylon.

The fourth scene of the prophecy explains how we will heal ourselves individually and collectively so we can integrate our bodies, spirits and souls and all that we create in into one spiritual reality the prophecy refers to as, "The New Holy City of Jerusalem". This final scene of the prophecy explains the end game of life for all of us.

An even more important message that comes from the prophecy and the parables of the Bibles New Testament is the Law of Creation and how it works through our body, spirit and soul.

All the parables of Jesus are explained through the four scenes of this prophecy; they explain how our spirit and soul evolve from dark, to light, to the bright light, and then to God; the oneness of pure consciousness.

The parables contained in the four books of the New Testament (the books of Matthew, Mark, Luke and John) tell the same story of healing that is the message of the prophecy. Each of these books has chapters and parables that explain how our spirit and soul work in a dark, light and bright reality of creation. Each chapter tells a story about the physical reality related to the parable that explains how creation (the spirit and soul) works.

The parables of the book of Matthew explain the reality of creation in the dark, light and bright realities of creation.

The parables of the book of Mark explain the reality of creation in the light and bright realities of creation.

The parables of the book of Luke explain the reality of creation in the bright realities of creation.

The parables of the book of John explain the reality of creation in the pure consciousness of God consciousness which the prophecy refers to as the New Holy City of Jerusalem.

The story explained through the prophecy and these four books of the New Testament are about the healing processes that re-create the collective spirit of mankind. Through our individual efforts and life's experiences we heal and re-create ourselves individually and the collective spirit of mankind.

This healing process is evolutionary. As we evolve through these processes of creation we will become one being of pure consciousness in body, spirit and soul. This is a reality that exists in all of our lives individually and collectively.

The first couple of chapters with parables in each of the four books of the New Testament talk about the Son of Man. The Son of Man is the collective spirit and soul of mankind. Then they talk about a broken spirit and the how that broken spirit exists in and grows beyond it spiritual existence in what is commonly referred to as a dark, light or bright state of mind. The book of John focuses its information on the highest state of mind – Pure consciousness or God consciousness.

Many people believe the prophecy predicts future events. It does not.

It explains creation and how it worked throughout history.

It explains how creation works through us in our day to day lives.

It gives us messages about how we can navigate through creation in an effort to make this world a better place.

He who can hear should listen. It will speak to you.

PREFACE

The Roman Catholic Church wrote the book called the Bible. The Bible contains the beliefs that today are the guiding principles of the many religions. Whether Roman Catholic, Catholic, Christian, Protestant, Lutheran, Presbyterian Baptist etc.., the Bible used to guide your beliefs has the same basic information and comes from the same sources of information. That source of information has a history steeped in the history of the tribes and nations of the Middle East and the Roman Empires strategies to manage and control them.

Two thousand years ago was a very dark time in mankind's history. The Roman Empire controlled the Middle East and Europe (approximately 2,500,000 square miles of land mass) for more than 500 years before the Catholic Church was created. Approximately 30 years before the Roman Empire formed the Roman Catholic Church, the empire was divided into dioceses. The emperor Diocletes wanted to change the way the empire was constructed. Diocletes transformed the empire from a collection of nations and tribes into Dioceses. This meant that people in the Middle East that were used to their tribe or nation being called Phoenicia or Persia were now given new names and borders. This was a very significant change for the people of the Middle East.

Until this point in time the Roman Empire respected the desires of the people of the Middle East to maintain their land and their spiritual beliefs (their beliefs in their own God(s)). These changes marked the beginning of Rome's desire to create the spirit of the Roman Empire. Diocletes placed Bishops as governors over the Dioceses and then 30 years later these Bishops became the Catholic Church. The Empire gave the church its charter which was to transform the spirit of the nation from a segmented set of spiritual beliefs with each nation and their own God or God's into one God, the God of the Roman Empire. They wanted the empire to have one God – the collective spirit of the Roman Empire. This was the beginning of the beliefs that there is only one God. Back in that time the Roman's had their beliefs in their God's and the Egyptians, Greeks, Phoenicians, Persians, Celtics, Germans, Irish etc. all had their own collection of Gods that they worshipped. These God's were the spirit of their tribe or nation. They were the spirit they created through their collective thoughts, words and actions. When the Roman Empire needed to control the spirit of all the people of the empire they empowered these Bishops to perform an almost impossible task. This was the original charter of the Roman Catholic Church. The first step in integrating all these different beliefs was to try to combine all the various beliefs that existed at that point in time into one book – The Bible. All of the various beliefs that existed in Europe and the Middle East at that point in time are contained in the Bible. But there was one set of beliefs that were not allowed to be taught throughout the empire; the truth about creation and how our body, spirit and soul create the spirit of our existence. The Roman Empire had very effectively controlled people's ability to create by taking the willpower of people from them and then forcing a system of creation into their lives. On one had it was a brilliant way to manage people and create the empire through the spirit of so many people but on the other hand it was an abomination that destroyed our ability to create a healthy way of life.

The Bishops and many spiritual leaders throughout the Empire at that time new the truths about creation and how it worked but also knew it was political suicide to teach them.

So, they wrote these truths into the Bible in the Book of Genesis, the parables of the New Testament and the symbols and images of the prophecy, "The Revelation of Christ".

Un-coding the images and symbols of these parts of the Bible will release the ancient knowledge and teachings of the past.

This book will give you these secrets which have been hidden for 2,000 years.

There are several keys that unlock the truths about the prophecy "The Revelation of Christ". They are:

1) The phrase, "I heard thunder and lightning and voices" – marks the end of one scene (time in the generation of a new collective reality) and the beginning of the next.
2) The angels in seven churches, seven angels with seven trumpets and seven cups – The seven parts of the spirit of mankind and all that is natural. They also represent the collective spirit of mankind.
3) The 12 parts of the Son of Man, the book with seven seals and the dragon and beast with seven heads – The soul of mankind (or a person) in the appropriate part of the kingdom of the heavens. They are the collective consciousness of mankind when the collective spirit is not capable of holding light and learning to hold light.
4) The 12 tribes of Israel, the 12,000 members of each tribe and the 144,000 people that make up the nation of Israel and the phrase and there were multitude of peoples and tongues and tribes and nations – describes the structure of the collective spirit of mankind.
5) Riddles hide the truths of each of these times in the history of mankind's evolution. The word mystery is at the beginning of a riddle, which when interpreted, explains the images and symbols of a scene.

The keys to unlocking the truths about the book of Genesis are:

1) Genesis is about how God created Creation and Evolution.
2) The first chapter is about creating the kingdom of the Heavens (the source of all that is natural in life).
3) At the end of the third chapter Adam and Eve are clothed in skin so the spirit and soul can have a human experience.
4) In the second chapter God breathes life into the soul of man and a complete being is formed.
5) In the first chapter God creates man in his image (this is when the spirit of man was created).
6) After the spirit and soul (a complete being) is created Adam falls into a deep sleep, this is a spiritual state of depression. This is when the first broken spirit occurred.
7) When he woke from this deep sleep Eve had been created. Now the collective spirit of mankind began. The collective male and female are the spirits of Adam and Eve.
8) They eat an apple and lose their light. The apple came from the tree of the knowledge of good and evil. In the prophecy the book with seven seals is the book of knowledge of love and light. When we lose our ability to love and forgive our spirit and soul is sealed away from this knowledge of love and light. To love our ability to love and forgive is to begin to feed off the knowledge of good and evil. To eat the apple from the tree of knowledge of good and evil is when your spirit and soul feed off this knowledge.
9) The fourth thru the fiftieth chapters of the book of Revelations chronicles the beginning of the spirit and souls human experience.
10) When Cain became jealous of Abel the seventh church of the prophecy, envy, was created.

The keys to understanding the parables of the New Testament and the prophecy are:

1) The parables in sequence tell the same story as the prophecy.
2) Each chapter and the parable within it explain how the body, spirit and soul work in creation.
3) The numbers that are either one digit like the number "1", numbers with a digit and a "0" like the number "10", numbers with a digit and two "0's" like the number "100" and finally numbers with a digit like the number "1" and three "0's" like the number "1,000" mean something significant. These numbers relate to the evolution of a person's spirit. Going from the lowest place in the evolutionary scale with the number 1 (like the parable of the lost son), to the next level of the scale where a person is learning to forgive and love again (like the parable of the 10 lost coins) to the next level on the scale which is living with and maintaining your love and light (like the lost sheep that leaves the other 100 sheep). The number 1,000 refers to expanding beyond the kingdom of the heavens into an angelic realm.

The prophecy is about the evolution of the collective spirit of mankind through creation. It is about how our spirit and soul evolve individually and collectively through creation. Another way of saying this is that it is about the evolution of the collective spirit of mankind and the consciousness that follows. Where the spirit goes the soul follows is an important state of nature or reality that exists in everyone's lives. Your spirit is a connection to feelings and emotions and your soul feeds you thoughts and consciousness. This is the foundation in a reality called emotion based consciousness.

Some examples that explain how a chapter and the parable within it explain the parable is below:

Chapter 13 of the book of Matthew explains how creation works in the kingdom of the heavens. It has several parables that explain creation and how it works through us.

THE SOWER (Matthew 13:1 – 13:9)

"In that day Jesus went out of the house, and sat by the sea. And many multitudes came together to him so that he entered a ship and sat down, and the whole multitude stood on the shore. And he spoke many things to them in parables, saying: Behold, the sower went forth to sow. And, as he sowed, some fell by the way, and the birds came and ate them up. But others fell on rocky places where they had not much earth; and they immediately sprung up because they had no depth of earth; but when the sun had risen, they I were scorched, and because they had no root they withered. But others fell on thorns, and the thorns grew up and choked them. But others I fell on good ground, and brought forth fruit, one a hundredfold, one sixty, one thirty. He that has ears, let him hear."

When a person tries to create in a darker reality his or her attempts to create will fail because a hardened hearts will not create. It is like planting a seed on hard rock; the sun will burn the life out of the love that should promote the growth from within the seed.

When a person begins to open his or her heart and so the seeds of life can grow from within them the reality that his or her heart still has no fertilization in it will not allow the love and light of a healthy seed to grow from within them.

When a person has some light in his or her spirit but not the complete light that is needed promote healthy growth; the seeds that are planted will grow but the thorns of the reality in a person's life will choke the life out of the plant that tries to grow. When a person tries to live a life that is positive and loving it is like you are learning how to live in a collective spirit that is still negative. The forces at work will make it very difficult to maintain your light when the collective is trying to exist without it.

When the collective spirit of mankind evolves into the bright light of the heavens and we all live with light in our spirit's and love in our hearts we will produce the fruits of our labor and we will feed off the fruits of our labor. This is when our collective evolution will bring peace on earth.

When the Bible talks about time and the end of time it is talking about the evolution of mankind's collective spirit through the dark of night, lesser light, greater light and light of day which are the four realities described in this parable.

WHY JESUS SPOKE IN PARABLES (Matthew 13:10 – 13:23)

"And the disciples came and said to him: Why speakest thou to them in parables? And he answered and said: Because to you it is given to know the mysteries of the kingdom of the heavens, but to them it is not given. For whoever has, to him shall be given, and he shall have abundance; but whoever has not, even that which he has shall be taken from him. For this reason I speak to them in parables, because when seeing they see not, and when hearing they hear not, neither do they understand. And in them is fulfilled the prophecy of Isaiah which says: By hearing you shall hear, and shall not understand, and seeing you shall see, and shall not perceive. For the heart of this people has become fat, and with their ears they hear heavily, and their eyes they have closed, lest perhaps they should see with their eyes, and hear with their ears and understand with their heart, and turn, and I should restore them to health. But blessed are your eyes, for they see, and your ears, for they hear.

Verily I say to you: Many prophets and righteous men desired to see what you see, and saw not, and to hear what you hear, and heard not. Hear you then the parable of him that sowed. When any one hears the word of the kingdom, and understands it not, the wicked one comes and snatches away that which is sown in his heart. This is he that was sown by the way. But he that was sown on the rocky places is he that hears the word, and immediately with joy receives it; yet he has no root in himself, but endures for a while; and when affliction or persecution arises because of the word, he immediately takes offense. But he that was sown among thorns is he that hears the word, and the care of the age and the deceitfulness of riches choke the word, and he becomes unfruitful. But he that was sown on good ground, is he that hears the word and understands it, who also bears fruit, and produces, one a hundred fold, one sixty, one thirty."

When Jesus explains why he spoke in parables; he is saying that in order to understand you must perceive. When a person or the collective spirit of mankind lives or exists in a dark reality our ability to perceive is limited or non-existent. In a darker reality we are only able to see with our eyes and hear with our ears. As we create light in our spirit we gain the sensitivity and sensing skills needed to sense or feel the spirit of his words. With the ability to sense the spirit of his words we can then perceive in order to understand.

Today, mankind has collectively evolved into a lesser light and many people are growing beyond the lesser light. Since we are collectively evolving, the collective spirit is now capable of gaining access to the consciousness that exists in this level of light.

PARABLE OF THE WEEDS (Matthew 13:24 – 13:30)

"Another parable laid he before them, saying: The kingdom of the heavens is likened to a man that sowed good seed in his field. But while the men slept, his enemy came and sowed tares over in the midst of the wheat and went away. But when the blade sprung up and produced fruit, then appeared the tares also. And the servants of the master of the

house came and said to him; Sir, didst thou not sow good seed in thy field? Whence then has it tares? He said to them: An enemy did this. And the servants say to him: Wilt thou then that we go and gather them up? But he said: No, lest perhaps while gathering the tares you root up the wheat together with them. Let both grow together till the harvest, and in time of harvest I will say to the reapers: Gather first the tares, and bind them into bundles to burn them; but gather the wheat into my granary."

This parable has a lot to do with the reality of the time that mankind is entering currently. It is about a time when the collective spirit of mankind exists with a dark, light and bright reality in our spirits. When mankind's collective spirit exists with some people capable of living in a state of mind where we are learning to love while others are not capable of this love and light it will be like living amongst the weeds that are in our garden. A harvest will exist when we will be able to separate the wheat from the weeds. Those that still need to learn more about living with love and light will stay in this transitional reality where they will continue to learn to love while those that learn to love completely will evolve into a reality where others will have the same love and light.

PARABLE OF THE MUSTARD SEED & YEAST (Matthew 13:31 – 13:35)

"Another parable laid he before them, saying: The kingdom of the heavens is like a grain of mustard, which a man took and sowed in his field: which indeed is less than all the seeds; but when it has grown, is greater than the garden plants, and becomes a tree, so that the birds of heaven come and roost in its branches. Another parable spoke he to them: The kingdom of the heavens is like leaven, which a woman took and hid in three measures of flour, till the whole was leavened. All these things spoke Jesus to the multitudes in parables, and without a parable spoke he nothing to them, that it might be fulfilled that was spoken through the prophet Isaiah, saying: I will open my mouth in parables, I will utter things concealed from the foundation."

No matter how small the thought, word or action; no matter how little love or light that is committed to them; the reality is that it will grow. Even the smallest seed will eventually grow. The most humble of thoughts will have the greatest growth over time.

PARABLE OF THE WEEDS EXPLAINED (Matthew 13:36 – 13:43)

"Then dismissing the multitudes he came into the house. And his disciples came to him, saying: Explain to us the parable of the tares of the field. And he answered and said: He that sows the good seed is the Son of man: the field is the world: the good seed, these are the sons of the kingdom; but the tares are the sons of the wicked one: the enemy that sowed them is the devil: the harvest is the conclusion of the age, and the reapers are angels. As then the tares are collected and burned in fire, so shall it be in the conclusion of the age. The Son of man shall send forth his angels, and they shall gather out of his kingdom all things that cause offense, and them that do iniquity, and shall cast them into the furnace of fire: there shall be weeping and gnashing of teeth. Then shall the righteous shine forth as the sun in the kingdom of their Father. He that has ears, let him hear.

Previously these parables spoke about the kingdom of the heavens. Now it talks about the kingdom of their father. When people get to the point where they are capable of growing beyond the kingdom of the heavens we will then evolve into what Revelations refers to as the New Holy City of Jerusalem or the kingdom of God (their father).

The end of age and the end of time are similar but subtly different. The end of a time is when we collectively grow from dark to light or from light to bright. The end of age is when we have learned what we need to learn from our experiences in the kingdom of the heavens and then evolve beyond it. What we are supposed to learn is how to love and maintain that love and light in our spirits. The kingdom of the heavens is all about emotions and consciousness and how we can learn to live with these emotions and the consciousness that comes with them. After we have learned to live with love and top use the consciousness that allows us to maintain our love and light we are ready to move on to a better place with new and greater challenges.

PARABLE OF THE HIDDEN TREASURE & THE PEARL (Matthew 13:44 – 13:46)

"The kingdom of the heavens is like treasure hid in the field, which a man found and hid, and for joy over it he went and sold all that he had, and bought that field. Again: the kingdom of the heavens is like a man, a merchant seeking goodly pearls: when he had found one pearl of great value, he went and sold all that he had and bought it."

The treasure chest is our emotions and the pearls inside it are the consciousness that comes with the emotions. Also hidden within our emotions and consciousness are spiritual gifts. When we evolve into a greater light we find deeper more positive emotions. When we open ourselves to these emotions we will find a greater consciousness within them. When we have learned to use these emotions and higher consciousness we will find the spiritual gifts that we can use to live with greater purpose in our lives.

PARABLE OF THE NET (Matthew 13:47 – 13:58)

"Again: the kingdom of the heavens is like a net that was cast into the sea and gathered of every kind: which, when it was full, they drew to the shore, and sitting down they gathered the good into baskets, but threw the bad away. So shall it be in the conclusion of the age: the angels shall come forth, and separate the wicked from among the righteous, and shall cast them into the furnace of fire: there shall be weeping and gnashing of teeth. Have you understood all these things? They say to him, Yes. And he said to them: Therefore, every scribe instructed in the kingdom of the heavens is like a man, a master of a house, who brings forth out of his treasury things new and old. And it came to pass, when Jesus had made an end of these parables, he departed thence. And he came into his own country, and taught them in their synagogue, so that they were astonished and said: Whence has this man this wisdom and the mighty works? Is not this the son of the carpenter? Is not his mother called Mary, and his brothers, James, and Joseph, and Simon, and Judah? And his sisters, are they not all with us? Whence then has this man all these things? And they were offended at him. But Jesus said to them, A prophet is not without honor unless in his own country and in his own house. And he did not many mighty works there because of their unbelief." (Matthew 13:1 – 13:58)

While this sounds like a process that exists where angels will sift through the good and evil of the world; it is not quite like that. It is more like a reality that exists where the good and the evil, the light and the dark will just naturally separate. The net is like a filter that separates the healthy and unhealthy spirits. It is something that happens naturally as a person evolves into a greater light and higher consciousness it is only natural that the two will separate as a person with brighter light continues on his or her path to enlightenment. As you will learn towards the end of this book this whole process is about creating an angel. When we become whole again and the broken spirit is healed we will exist with the light of an angel. An angel is a being of light that is pure in intention. When we learn to exist with such a great sense of purpose that we feel as if there is nothing else that matters other than to do what just comes naturally, we will know what it feels like to be angelic in nature.

Another example of how a parable that is explained by understanding the chapter it is written in is:

> *"And the disciples having come to the other side had forgotten to take bread. And Jesus said to them: Take heed and beware of the leaven of the Pharisees and Sadducees. And they reasoned among themselves, saying: Because we took no bread. But Jesus perceiving it, said: Why reason among yourselves, O you of little faith, because you took no bread? Do you not yet understand, and do you not remember the five loaves of the five thousand, and how many traveling baskets you took up? nor the seven loaves of the four thousand, and how many provision baskets you took up? How is it that you do not understand that I spoke not to you of bread? But beware of the leaven of the Pharisees and Sadducees. Then they understood that he did not bid them beware of the leaven of the Pharisees and the Sadducees, but of the teaching of the Pharisees and Sadducees. (Matthew 16:5 – 16:12)*

This parable is about people feeding off the spirit of the words of others. When someone tells you something and you believe what they say and then act on their guidance you are creating your life based on what others say. We need to trust ourselves and our inner voice and learn to feed our spirit by doing what we know is the right thing to do, not what others tell us is best for us. Especially when we know that others do not have our best interest in mind when they try to guide us to do what is best for them. When we feed off of the words of others we are creating what they want us to do. We are not feeding our spirit and soul we are feeding theirs.

When others create the spirit of their words and they can assert their will onto others. When we accept (especially passionately accept) their words we are accepting the spirit of their words; then we create a bond with them. This bond is a spiritual bond that can lead to being controlling in nature. It can control you because it can impact your spirit and then your feelings. When your emotions and feelings are impacted by others (especially a large group of people all with the same acceptance of someone else's spirit) you become one with this collective spirit. I hope you can see how this can become very controlling and have a big impact on you and on your life. When a large group of people accept the spirit of a person's words it can have a big impact on that person's life also. If a person creates an anger based spirit and then a lot of people that have an anger based reality in their life accept him into their reality he can then become consumed by their spirits also.

As you read this book you will learn:

1) What the collective spirit is and how it works.
2) What the collective consciousness is and how it works.
3) That creation and evolution are two parts of an intricate system of which we are only one part. You will learn that creation is about creating the spirit of your thoughts, words and actions.
4) That the Bible is a book that explains how creation works and the evolution of creation.
5) How we work as individuals to re-create the collective spirit of mankind and the collective consciousness.
6) How our body, spirit and soul works in a state of mind commonly referred to as being broken. In this state of mind our body, spirit and soul repel each other and create an anger based reality in our lives.
7) How our body, spirit and soul works in a state of mind commonly referred to as being healed or unified as one being in love and light consciousness. In this state of mind our body, spirit and soul attract each other and create a love based reality in our lives.
8) How our individual spirit and soul are impacted by the collective spirit and collective consciousness and how the collective spirit and consciousness are impacted by each and every one of us.

INTRODUCTION

The prophecy tells three stories simultaneously:

1) The history of the collective spirit and consciousness of mankind.
2) The law and processes of creation that create our spirit and consciousness.
3) How this law of creation and its processes will transform our spirit and consciousness into new realities from generation to generation and lifetime to lifetime.

The Catholic Bible tells the same three stories.

- The book of Genesis tells the story of mankind collectively in the beginning of our time.
- The Old Testament tells the story of how the collective spirit mankind manifested in the lives of the Israelites and others in the Middle East as mankind lived in a darker reality. The story called Exodus is the story of the beginning of creation (when Moses demonstrated unconditional love for the Israelites). Moses had a plan to help the Israelites but it did not go according to plan and creation took a wrong turn
- The New Testament tells the story of Jesus when he came to fix the plan to use creation to heal the Israelites and mankind.

The original intention of the writers of the Bible was to write these three stories about creation and how it works so this knowledge would be preserved despite the direction of the Roman Empire. It was the Roman Empires need to create the spirit of the Roman Empire that they referred to as one God that motivated them to create the Catholic Church. The church was empowered to lead the empire in an attempt to create the spirit of the empire. This collective spirit is where the concept of one God originated. It was the empires intention to transform all the various peoples of the empire and their collective spirit's (their God's) into the collective spirit of the Roman Empire. There was nothing wrong with this after all they did rule 2,500,000 square miles of land mass and had to find a way to unite them. After 500 years of ruling over Europe and the Middle East they finally tried to unite them as one collective spirit. The Catholic Church was empowered to complete this task. The church had to accomplish this task while at the same time do what the leaders of the empire told them to do. The empire did not want people to know the true power of their individual spirits. This is why these truths about evolution and creation were hidden in the code of the Bible. These truths are explained in this book and the series that explain the prophecy "The Revelation of Christ".

The prophecy Revelations tells the entire story of the collective spirit and soul of mankind from when it began through the days of Moses, Exodus, Jesus and ends with a description of how mankind someday will evolve into pure consciousness; God consciousness. The prophecy refers to this pure state of mind as, "The New Holy City of Jerusalem".

In order to understand Revelations you have to understand the entire Bible. Interpreting the images and symbols of the prophecy is the key to understanding the entire Bible. The best way to explain this is to begin at the beginning, Genesis.

GENESIS

In the beginning God created creation and then let his creation evolve through creation. In this way creation and evolution are two intricately linked realities of one another. They are intricately linked through time. In order to understand creation you have to understand evolution; and, in order to understand evolution you have to understand creation. Creation occurs constantly throughout our lives. Creation exists as a moment in time; as a moment in evolution. Evolution exists to allow creation to occur over time. In the beginning God created the heavens and the earth and then let it be. The words, "Let it be" means to let that which was created to evolve into what it should be in order for it to achieve that which it is meant to be. The last phrase in this process of creation is that God made something. This is the last step of the process of creation. The process of creation begins with creating the spirit and then letting the spirit of that which was created evolve and then if a physical reality is needed it will be (or made) as creation and evolution work together to create what should be throughout time.

Question: This gives new insight into the age old question – Which came first the chicken of the egg?

Answer: A need had to exist and then the spirit of the chicken would have created the spirit of the chicken and then the chicken evolved through evolution.

In the beginning the need for a physical life had to exist. The existence of dark and light was the first reality that existed. Then the heavens were created to allow a spiritual bridge to exist so dark spirit could transform itself into light through a human experience. Nature and its physical existence as the earth, stars, sun and moon was created first. Then animals were created and finally man was needed to allow the original purpose of creation to come to fruition.

The first day of Genesis describes the first generation of the creation of creation. Heaven and Earth are created and darkness is over the deep and the spirit of God moved upon the waters. On this first generation of creation the light was separated from the dark. It is very important to recognize that the purpose of creation was to create a bridge that will allow dark spirit to experience that which it needs to evolve from dark to light. The kingdom of the heavens is the bridge that will create that which is needed to transform dark to light.

The second day of creation is the generation of the firmament which separates the water from the waters. As creation evolved the firmament separated the light of day from the dark of night. What is significant about this second day of creation is that nothing was created. God let the firmament be, what is should be and then it made its place in the heavens. All is good in creation when evolution and creation work together.

On the third day God, "let" (evolution continued) the earth, waters (seas and rivers and streams) "be" what they should be in spirit so the evolution of creation could continue.

On the fourth day evolution continues as heavenly bodies are allowed to be what they should be.

The significance of this reality of the book of Genesis is that this creation is a perfect correlation to some of the images and symbols of the prophecy Revelations. As you read on you will learn that the evolution of the spirit of nature and the collective spirit of mankind is explained through seven angels that have seven trumpets and seven angels that hold seven cups. The first four angels describe events that impact the earth, seas, rivers and streams and heavenly bodies (sun, moon and stars), respectively.

The body, spirit and soul of mankind's existence occurred through the same processes of creation. First God created man in his image and then let the soul of man be and then Adam and Eve were clothed in skin so the spirit and soul could have a human experience. The earth, seas, rivers and streams and heavenly bodies all evolved through the same process of creation. As all of nature evolved from the same original creation we are all linked together as one in spirit. Throughout this book you will learn it is only natural that there are seven parts to the spirit of mankind and seven parts to each the elements of nature that were created in the beginning. It is through this seven sided matrix that man and nature exist together as one in nature. An important phrase in the prophecy states that "the third part of nature or man" is impacted by events described in the prophecy. This third part of man and nature refers to a reality of evolution that will end when the third part of the spirit of man and nature is re-created. The event that will end the destructive nature of mankind's existence is when we create a deep rooted love of family within our lives. Love of family is the answer. As you will learn while reading this book the reason the story of the family of Israel was chosen to tell the story of mankind's evolution is because of the conflict between Israel and Islam. While there are many similar stories that exist in all nations it is the story of the broken spirit of the Israelites when the founding father of the Israelites had to send his first born and mother into the desert alone. From that day forward (about 3,700 years ago until today) the broken spirits of both Israel and Islam have not felt the love for one another that their families deserve to share. As you will learn there is a healing event that occurs when people forgive one another. Only when these two nations create a forgiving spirit between themselves will the spirit of mankind be whole again. This forgiveness will happen someday in the future and when it does it will be the Holiest of all events.

REVELATIONS

The prophecy, "The Revelations of Christ" contains four scenes. Each scene contains images and symbols that describe these scenes. The first three scenes contain a riddle that explains the scene. The riddles are identified by the word "mystery".

THE FIRST SCENE CONTAINS

In the beginning there was Adam (a complete being in spirit and soul was created) and then there was Adam and Eve (the first broken spirit):

a. the son of man walking among 7 candle sticks
b. the 7 churches
c. the mystery of the seven stars, 7 angels, seven candlesticks and 7 churches

THE SECOND SCENE CONTAINS

Then there was man (Adam and Eve are now clothed in skin) and the collective spirit and soul of mankind as we journeyed into a darker spiritual reality. Moses demonstrates unconditional love for the Israelites and released the seals that sealed their fate:

a. the lamb (the evolution of mankind)
b. the book with 7 seals (the book of the knowledge of dark and light)
c. the 7 angels with 7 trumpets
d. the 12 tribes of 12,000 members per tribe that are the 144,000 that are sealed by the 7 seals
e. the mystery of the angel with the little book that tastes sweet in ST. John's mouth but turns bitter in his stomach

THE THIRD SCENE CONTAINS

Mankind's evolution from the days of Moses up to and after the time of Jesus:

a. the woman about to give birth to a child
b. a dragon waiting to consume the child (has 7 heads and 10 horns)
c. a beast that rises up from the sea with similar characteristics as the dragon (has 7 heads and 10 horns)
d. a beast that comes from the earth (looks like a lamb and has 2 horns)
e. the lamb and the 144,000 and the great winepress
f. the 7 angels with 7 cups
g. the mystery of Babylon

THE FOURTH SCENE CONTAINS

Our eventual evolution into pure consciousness - The new holy city of Jerusalem

    a. its foundations
        i. There are 12 foundations
        ii. each foundation has the name of the 12 Apostles written on them
        iii. each foundation is adorned in 1 of 12 crystals
    b. its walls
        iv. there are 4 walls each having 3 gates
        v. these walls are 12,000 cubits wide and 12,000 cubits high
        vi. the city is 144,000 cubits long

IN THE BEGINNING (THE FIRST SCENE IN THE PROPHECY AND THE BOOK OF GENESIS FROM THE BIBLE)

CREATION

The prophecy begins with the image of the son of man; Adam from the book of Genesis. When Adam was first created he was a complete being. This meant that he was whole (Holy) and fully integrated in body and spirit. All of nature and creation were there for him to use to enjoy but it was not enough and he fell into a deep sleep. When a complete being in spirit and soul goes to sleep it is like a person having depression; it is dead to creation. To be dead to creation is to have no life in spirit, it is like there is no rhythm or vibration in your spirit and therefore you cannot express yourself; therefore you cannot create and are dead to creation.

The complete being in love and light falls into a deep depression and awakens to find that his spirit and soul have split and he is now no longer lonely; Adam and Eve are now born in spirit. Adam is the soul and Eve is the spirit. They now exist as two separate parts of the same whole being but are not complete as one in pure consciousness. The son of man has now transformed itself into a broken spirit (the soul or Adam) walking among seven candlesticks and the seven churches (the spirit or Eve). At this step in the evolution The Son of Man is the collective soul (collective consciousness) and the seven churches are the seven parts of the collective spirit. When the prophecy says the Son of Man is seen as walking among seven candlesticks he is walking in the darker reality of the kingdom of the heavens. These seven candlesticks are not lit and this is why it is about the darker side of mankind's collective consciousness.

The best way to describe the spirit and soul is to try to imagine a cloud with an angel on it. The spirit is the cloud and the soul is the angel. Where the cloud goes the angel has to follow; therefore where the spirit goes the soul has to follow. Just like after Eve ate the apple from the tree of knowledge of good and evil Adam did also. This is because where one goes the other has to follow. In a similar way there is another image later in the prophecy where a rider on a horse named death is followed closely by Hades. When the spirit dies the soul follow it into the darker reality that comes from the kingdom of the heavens. This is when mankind created hell on earth. This image explains how the spirit and soul dis-evolve into the darkness of the abyss.

The seven churches represent the seven parts of the spirit broken. They are churches because a church is the home of your spirit and soul. When a spirit and soul are broken they exist in a darker reality. This is why the soul (son of man) is seen walking among seven candlesticks. These seven candlesticks are not lit. With no flame to guide us, we are living in the darker reality of life. With the spirit and soul existing in darkness the seven churches also represent the darker reality of our emotional connection to life. These seven churches are the seven deadly sins:

1) Wrath
2) Greed
3) Lust
4) Gluttony
5) Sloth
6) Pride
7) Envy

THE EVOLUTION OF MANKIND (THE REST OF THE BIBLE AND THE REST OF THE PROPHECY)

The second scene of the prophecy is where mankind evolves and expands as the spirit and soul now become the body, spirit and soul. After Adam and Eve ate the apple from the tree of the knowledge of good and evil they are clothed in skin and begin the journey we call life.

The prophecy says that the angels and other forces of creation are searching for someone, a lamb. They are searching for the next piece of the puzzle that is needed in order for creation to work; they are searching for mankind to evolve so we can help fix the broken spirit that is Adam and Eve; that is our lives. Mankind is the lamb. The lamb is also any person that evolves to a greater spiritual level at any point in time. Moses and Jesus are examples of an individual person that is the lamb. Moses demonstrated unconditional love for the Israelites and released the seals so creation could become a greater reality in the lives of the Israelites and all of mankind. Moses had a plan to help the Israelites but was not able to complete his part of the plan; Jesus came to put the plan back on track.

The prophecy and the Bible tell the story of mankind's evolution in body, spirit and soul. Since these three component parts of our existence are what the prophecy is about, its images and symbols have to tell several stories at the same time. For example the missing link in nature is mankind but the missing link in creation is about the spirit and soul. Therefore these angels and guides of creation that are searching for someone, are searching for mankind to evolve in nature and then for mankind to evolve spiritually in creation. When Moses demonstrates unconditional love for the Israelites he released the seven seals that sealed mankind's fate into the darkness of the abyss; then when Jesus came he planted the seeds of unconditional love and forgiveness in the collective spirit of mankind. This was like planting a seed in the unfertile soil of the spirit of mankind that, today, has grown into the creation of forgiveness in many of our lives. I hope you can now see that there are many layers of the prophecy just like there are many layers to our existence. The missing links in nature and creation are:

1) Mankind (missing link in nature)
2) Moses demonstrating unconditional love (missing link in creation)
3) Jesus planting the seed of forgiveness in the collective spirit of mankind (missing link in creation)

The images and symbols of the prophecy also tell the story of an individual person's body, spirit and soul and the collective spirit and collective consciousness of mankind. It tells our story as we individually and collectively evolve through creation and transform the collective spirit and soul of mankind from dark to light to bright to pure consciousness.

As mankind evolved there were more and more people living with greater degrees of broken spirits. This reality of life is about how we live our lives with hardships and then our spirit breaks into several pieces. In the past, many thousands of years ago the hardships were much greater than they are today. In this worse state of mind a broken spirit might have meant that a person's spirit was broken into many pieces.

Question: What happens to all these pieces after a person dies?

Answer: Those broken pieces take on a life of their own.

This means that if a person's spirit is broken into 10 pieces there will be 10 people that will exist in future life-times each with a smaller spirit and soul and a diminished capacity to create. This process of breaking down a person's spirit is all a part of the processes of creation. This process of spiritual break-down continues until the spirit is capable of re-creating its-self.

The spirit and soul needs the body in order for the process of re-creation to work. It is only through the sensitivity that comes with feelings and emotions that our body, spirit and soul are capable of sensing the pain of hardships, sadness etc. Without the body the rationalization and acceptance of our actions and the pain we either feel or cause would not exist and the spirit and soul would not be motivated to change. When we accept that we are hurting others we have that something that is needed to reach deep into our spirit and soul so we can commit to changing our spirit and growing into a better reality in our physical lives.

As the prophecy continues from one scene to the next, each scene contains more images and symbols. This is because as mankind evolves through creation there are more people and more creations that evolve from life-time to life-time and generation to generation. The word generation is an interesting one because it has two meanings in the prophecy. In one sense it means a generation of people. It also means to generate a change. When the two meanings of this word are put together it means that generations of children will enter the world to create changes to the world. This will be discussed in greater detail in the third scene of the prophecy.

The first scene is about the creation of Adam and Eve and the second scene is about the evolution of mankind. It is the deep desire of those that are searching for the lamb that creates the spirit of the desire for mankind to evolve. Then it was the deep desires of the Israelites that brought Moses into their lives. The spirit of mankind comes from Adam and Eve and it will eventually evolve back into a spiritually stronger Adam. A spiritually stronger Adam is a complete being that will not suffer from the perceived hardship that created the original broken spirit.

This scene also includes a description of how mankind evolved in the beginning. There is a description of 12 tribes that each contained 12,000 people that made up a nation of 144,000 people that were sealed. This represented how mankind survived as families and tribes that were all part of a nation; the structure of the collective spirit that evolved through many lifetimes of hardships and broken spirits.

The numbers 1 and 2 are in reference to Adam becoming Adam and Eve.

The number 12,000 is also the numbers 1, 2 and 000. The number 12,000 represents the spiritual breakdown that evolved and the numbers 1, 2 and 000 represent the healing that will occur someday as we into 1 in body, spirit and soul.

The number 144,000 is also the numbers 1, 4, 4 and 000. The number 144,000 represents the complete breakdown of the spirit and soul into a much larger reality.

1) the number 1 represents the body
2) the first 4 represents the 4 loves that were lost as mankind dis-evolved
3) the second number 4 represents the four levels of consciousness that we will experience as we evolve back into a complete being through the heavens
4) the 000 simply represents becoming one in body, spirit and soul

There is still one more relationship that these numbers represent. The numbers 12, 12,000 and 144,000 represent the structure of the collective spirit of mankind. As 1 and then 2 that became 12,000 and then 1,444,000. In the beginning there was only Adam and then there was Adam and Eve. Now there are many billions of people that exist in body, spirit and soul. Back in the days of the prophecy the structure of the spirit of mankind existed as nations that consisted of tribes and tribes that consisted of families and families that consisted of people. The prophecy refers to the Israelites but the collective spirit of mankind at that point in time consisted of many nations; there were the Israelites, Islam, Greeks, Romans, Celtics, Germanics and more. All of these different cultures had a similar top down structure that included many Gods. The interesting reality though is that all the different cultures had similar God's (god of war, god of love, god of the arts etc.). These gods represented what this book refers to as the ambient spirits created by the collective spirit of the nation. The ambient spirits of our creation (or gods) are created by a large number (hundreds of thousands) of people that all feel the same feelings and do the same things. When a large number of people are all afraid they create the spirit of their fear within themselves then when they act on those fears they create the spirit of their fears in the air around them. Hundreds of thousands of people going to war would create the gods of war and the nation capable of channeling the greatest amount of aggression would be able to say that their god is greater than another nations. Today we no longer refer to these spiritual creations as god so I am referring to them as the ambient spirit of our creations.

Back in the days of the Roman Empire people from one nation did not talk with or associate with people from another nation. Members from one family rarely interacted with other families. The structure of the spirit of a nation was a function of the people that were in a family and the families within the tribes that made up the nation. Today, and for the past 100 years people from different countries have married one another, people from Germany and Italy, France and Germany, Spain and Portugal, America and Africa have all interacted with one another and even married one another. This is a significant change that exists within the structure of the spirit of the collective spirit of mankind. More recently the gay rights and bisexual marriages as well as transvestite and sex change operations are radically changing the structure of the collective spirit of mankind. This is what it means to be one in spirit.

The prophecy is about the evolution and creation of the body, spirit and soul. To fully understand both you have to start with creation and evolution. If we are going to start with creation and evolution we have to understand the Bible's book of Genesis. The first three chapters of the book of Genesis establish the creation of the body, spirit and soul.

Chapter 1 is about the spirit of man.
Chapter 2 is when the Lord God breathes life into the soul of man and a complete being is formed.
Chapter 3 is when Adam and Eve eat the apple from the tree of the knowledge of good and evil (when the spirit feeds off the knowledge of good and evil) and are clothed in skin (have a human experience).

In order to understand this perspective of creation and evolution you have to understand that God created, Let it be and then allowed what was created to be made a reality in a physical sense. The spirit of a deep rooted desire creates the spirit of that desire, then the consciousness of the spirit follows and then finally what is needed in reality will exist.

In chapter 1 of the book of Genesis God created the spirit of:

1) Heaven and Earth on the first day
2) Animals on the fifth day
3) Man in his own image on the sixth day

After each of these creations he let them be and they evolved into:

1) The dark of night and light of day on the first day
2) The firmament that separated the light of day from the dark of night on the second day
3) The Earth, waters, plants and trees and the seeds to grow them on the third day
4) The sun, moon and stars on the fourth day
5) Beasts on the sixth day

Finally God made the following:

1) The firmament on the second day
2) The greater light, the lesser light and the stars on the fourth day
3) The beasts of the earth on the sixth day

As the spirit of mankind evolves so does the spirit of all of creation, also all of creation was created to help and support the evolution of the spirit and soul of mankind. This reality is depicted in the prophecy's representation of the evolution of the spirit. The evolution of the collective spirit of mankind is illustrated in the first scene of the prophecy as seven angels in seven churches, in the second scene as seven angels with seven trumpets and the third scene as seven angels with seven cups. The first scene is about the creation of the seven parts of the broken spirit of mankind, the second and third scenes are about the evolution of the spirit of all that was created in the first chapter of Genesis. The first four angels (with trumpets and cups) are about:

1) The earth
2) seas – large bodies of water
3) rivers and streams
4) heavenly bodies

On the sixth day God created man and the sixth seal, trumpet and cup explain the evolution of the spirit and soul of mankind.

As you can see one of the keys to unfolding the mystery of the Bible is to read it like a matrix. It is a seven sided matrix that has the seven days of creation and the seven churches that define our spiritual reality. The prophecy explain that life is about how emotion based consciousness creates the reality that is our life and our lives. The darker our spirit the more anger in the reality of the life we create; the lighter our spirit the greater the love that will exist in the realities we create.

The scenes of the prophecy explain how the seven parts of your spirit evolve through creation as we grow from dark to light to bright and then into pure consciousness. The collective spirit grows in such a way as to help us to evolve and as we evolve we help it to heal and grow to its next level in evolution.

In creation the spirit and soul of mankind occurred on the sixth day of creation and the angel with the sixth trumpet and sixth cup is the angel of the sixth church; they tell the story of the evolution of mankind. Each of the angels with a trumpet or cup tells the story of the evolution of creation and how nature and creation work together to motivate and encourage us to re-create our-selves thereby creating the evolution of the collective spirit and soul of mankind and all of creation. The prophecy is telling us that mankind has a great influence over the spirit of all of nature.

HOW REVELATIONS EXPLAINS THE BOOK OF GENESIS

The first scene of the prophecy is about the son of man walking among seven candlesticks and seven churches. The first sentence of Genesis states that darkness was over the deep. The seven candlesticks are not lit; candlesticks that are not lit represent the darkness that existed in the beginning. The seven candlesticks define the darkness that a broken spirit lives in (the kingdom of the heavens) and the seven churches define the darkness of the spirit.

The second scene immediately talks about seven blazing lamps of fire ("there were seven lamps of fire burning before the throne, which are the seven spirits of God" (Rev. 5)). In Genesis God said let there be light. This light is represented by these lamps of fire. Now the prophecy has the darkness that is over the deep and the spirit of God that is over the waters. According to Genesis the dark was separated from the light and this was the end of the first day.

The second scene of the prophecy contains a book with seven seals and seven angels with seven trumpets. This book contains the knowledge of love and light that is sealed away from mankind's consciousness when our spirit is sealed away from the light, We create these seals when we are not strong enough in spirit to repent (forgive) and overcome (live with love) the hardships that occur in our lives. When Adam and Eve ate the apple it was from the tree of knowledge of good and evil. They are then clothed in skin and have a human experience to gain a greater understanding of both good and evil. The spirit and soul exist in a darker state of mind until we (in body, spirit and soul) are able to create a forgiving spirit. When a person begins his or her quest to find their light, they have to learn to create a spirit strong enough to hold light and then learn to live with love and then to share that love with others. This is what creation is all about. We do not go straight from having a dark spirit to living in the light. We have to go through a dimmer light area that Genesis refers to as the firmament. While transforming our spirits from dark to light we learn to forgive and live with love again. This book with seven seals is the firmament that divides the waters from the waters and separates the dark of night from the light of day. When on your journey into a darker reality the moments in your life define your existence; when you start you quest you begin to learn how to allow your spirit's existence to define the moments in your life.

On the next day of Genesis the land was formed and God called it the earth and then the seas were also formed. In this second scene of the prophecy there are also seven angels with seven trumpets. The first angel sounds his trumpet and hail, fire and blood were thrown into the earth. When the second angel sounds its trumpet a great mountain is cast into the sea. The third angel sounds its trumpet and a great star comes from heaven and falls upon the third part of the rivers and streams. On the third day of Genesis God made the trees and plants. There is not a strong correlation between Revelations and Genesis on this day.

On the fourth day of the genesis of creation God said let there be lights in the firmament of the heavens to divide the day from the night. These two lights are the greater light (Sun) and lesser light (moon) and he made the stars. In the prophecy the fourth angel sounds his trumpet and the third part of the sun, moon and stars are smitten.

The third scene of the prophecy also has seven angels but in this scene they pour cups onto the earth, seas, rivers and stream and the heavens.

This almost perfect correlation between the prophecy and the book of Genesis has to be understood when learning about creation, evolution, Genesis or the prophecy.

In the first scene of the prophecy there is the spirit and soul but man had not yet evolved. In the second scene there are angels searching for someone who can open the seven seals that seal the book. No one in heaven, or on the earth, or under the earth is able to open the book or look upon it. This is because the spirit and soul alone was not enough to experience life in such a way as to be able to re-create the darkness of the spirit that existed in the beginning. Then mankind evolved and the power of creation existed with human life. Without a human body the spirit and soul are not capable of experiencing and feeling that something that is necessary to commit to the process of transforming the spirit and soul from dark to light. The body is just as important to this process of transformation as the spirit and soul. The three have to work together in order to make the change that is the reason for our lives. This synchronicity is vital to the evolution of the body, spirit and soul as we attempt to fulfill God's purpose for creation and evolution.

This lamb that releases the seals has several meanings to the prophecy. The prophecy does more than just explain Genesis. It also tells the story of the evolution of the body, spirit and soul over time. In this part of the interpretation of the prophecy we learn that Moses releases the seals at a point in time when previously, no one had demonstrated unconditional love. When Moses demonstrated unconditional love for the Israelites the seals are released and the potential for mankind to create through the power of love and light was released into our lives. But the plan did not go according to plan and Jesus came to fix the problem with the collective spirit of mankind. Through his purpose to live with a passion to love and forgive Jesus planted these seeds of creation in the collective spirit of mankind and in the ambient spirit of mankind. This seed of forgiveness and love has been growing in our lives for many thousands of years and has finally begun to produce its fruit. As we learn to forgive and love we will co-create the spirit of love and forgiveness in the air around us as we create this ambient spirit of mankind's creation.

Throughout this book the word revelations will be used instead of the complete title of the prophecy "The Revelation of Christ".

MANIFESTATION VS CREATION

Thousands of years ago the ancient prophets used the word manifest to describe a completely different reality than what many people teach its meaning as today. In the past the word manifest meant that we manifest the spirit of our thoughts, words and actions. They were talking about how our thoughts, words and actions manifest (or create) the spirit of our thoughts words and actions. You need to understand that the spirit we create is a direct reflection of spirit in us (that we are) at the moment in time (moment in creation) when we say think or do anything (and everything). The best way to discuss the difference between creation and manifestation is to say that we create our personal spirit by being in a moment in which we are in a loving state of mind or in an anger based state of mind; and we manifest the aggression of compassion of that state of mind when we act on the thoughts and feelings we receive from that state of mind. I hope you can see that manifestation and creation are very similar realities in creation but very different in how we work as beings of light and dark.

In the past the ancient prophets taught people that their personal spirit manifests through them as they create the reality that is their life. When mankind's collective spirit manifests it is creating the lifestyle that exists in the world or in a part of the world. Collectively we manifest or create human nature. Human nature is a reflection of the collective spirit and consciousness of mankind. This is how our spirit and soul manifest through us. When we collectively feel or believe that people born with a certain color hair are (for example blonde hair) are better than those with another color hair; we create a feeling within the collective spirit of mankind that is a reflection of those thoughts. All people can then be impacted by the thought and feeling that they are better or not as good because of this collective creation. When a person creates his or her personal spirit to be strong enough to overcome the belief that hair color makes the person better or worse he or she has made a better reality for themselves and for others. When a person overcomes this reality of human nature they pave the way for others to follow their lead.

Thousands of years ago when hundreds of thousands of people felt afraid or were terrified by a neighboring nation they felt the fear that was their own collective spirit. They referred to this collective spirit that came from within them as God. Then when they acted on this fear and terror in an aggressive way and engaged in a war with their neighboring nation they created their god of war.

Today many people are teaching others that manifestation and creation are synonymous. They really are not. But to make it easier for readers that have this understanding of creation I am not using the term manifestation throughout this book. Throughout this book we will talk about how we create our personal spirit and then we create the spirit of our thoughts, words and actions.

Today people teach the following as a definition of manifestation.

Man manifests through a purposeful intention. Manifestation is man's deliberate and intentional use of the forces of nature and/or creation to <u>man-ifest</u> something we want or need. There are forces of nature and forces of creation; they are very different from the spirit of nature and spirit of creation. Forces of nature work within the spirit of nature and forces of creation work within the spirit of creation.

To manifest a feeling of love in your personal spirit is very different from re-creating your personal spirit into a love-based spirit. When we want or need others to like us we strive to make everyone like us. When we do this we manifest the spirit of love around us; but this is not our personal spirit. It is through our personal spirit that we create. This approach to manifesting is about forcing your will onto yourself or others in such a way as to make something physical appear in your life. When you manifest in this way you are using your wants and needs, desires and cravings to bring something or someone into your life so you can make your life easier or better in some way. This is not how to become one in body, spirit and soul. This is not how to synchronize our body, spirit and soul in such a way as to create a more harmonious way of life.

The ancient prophets were talking about a natural process that comes from your spirit and flows through you (through your body) as you create the reality that is your life.

THE THIRD TESTAMENT

Many people today talk about the third testament as a spiritual or religious book written by someone over the last 2,000 years. Some say the book of Mormon or the Koran should be the third testament to the Bible. As you read this book you may realize that it is time to add a new testament to the bible but it is not what most people think it should be. Although these other books should be a part of this testament they are not "**THE**" testament. A testament to someone or something is merely a way of honoring or adding value to someone or something that happens throughout history. To attest to something is to certify or bear witness to an event. For example the book of Genesis marks the beginning of a time in creation. It is when creation and evolution began. Then there is a time period that chronicles the events that occurred throughout time as a way to attest to what happened after this significant spiritual event. This time period is chronicled by 47 chapters in the book of Genesis that describe the evolution of mankind from the genesis of creation until the end of that time. Then there is the time of Moses. When Moses demonstrated unconditional love for the Israelites is the beginning of the second time in the history of the evolution of mankind. When Moses demonstrated unconditional love for the Israelites he released the seals that sealed the Israelites and all of mankind's fate into a darker reality. With the release of these seals creation became a reality in our lives. The Bibles book of Exodus chronicles the spiritual significance of the efforts of Moses and the Old Testament chronicles the historic events that occurred the death of Moses. The time of Moses ended when Jesus came. When Jesus lived with unconditional love and forgiveness he planted these seeds in the collective spirit of mankind. This began the third era or time of creation. This New Testament to the impact of the works of Jesus now need to be written to chronicle the events and realities of mankind since his death. It is the second part of the time period referred to as "The New Testament". When Jesus talks about the end of time he is referring to the end of this era or time in the spiritual evolution of the collective spirit of mankind and the historic events and experiences that occurred after it.

As mankind is now evolving into a higher spirit and greater consciousness we are entering another time in the evolution of the collective spirit of mankind.

This is why a new and improved of third testament must be written. As you read this book or the book "Revelations – Your Role in God's Plan to Replace Darkness with Light" you will see some of the significant events that occurred throughout the past 2,000 years that should be included in this third testament. Also included in this third testament are people that made a significant impact on mankind. Spiritual leaders like Mohammad, the Dalai Lamas, Gandhi, the Popes and others that have made a significant spiritual impact on the lives of many people and on the collective spirit of mankind need to be documented in this third testament. Experiences and events like the economics of greed that manifests in the 75 year cycle of depression also should be included in this part of the New Testament.

Then the Third Testament will discuss the significance of mankind's quest to find its light as we have created our own significant spiritual event because we have learned to forgive and love.

The prophecy, "The Revelations of Christ" has three scenes in it that are a mirror image of these three parts of the Bible.

The first scene is The Son of Man Walking among Seven Candlesticks and Seven Churches with an angel in each church. This is a reflection of Genesis and the story of Adam and Eve.

The second scene is a Book with Seven Seals that are released by a Lamb and Seven Angels sounding Seven Trumpets. This scene also introduces the families of Israel. This is about Moses demonstrating unconditional love; thereby releasing the seals that sealed the fate of the Israelites and all of mankind and the journey the Israelites took while living in the desert for 40 years and the coming of Jesus to help mankind get back on the right path to save our spirits individually and collectively.

The third scene is about a woman about to give birth to a child, a dragon waiting to consume the child, 2 beasts, a great wine press and seven angels filled with plagues holding seven cups. This scene is about the spiritual significance that occurred after Jesus came. This is the spiritual reality that will guide mankind until the end of this time in the evolution of the collective spirit and consciousness of mankind.

CHAPTER 1

THE GENESIS THAT WAS AND IS CREATION

In the beginning there was Adam (a complete being in spirit and soul was created) and then there was Adam and Eve (the first broken spirit)

THROUGHOUT THIS BOOK WE WILL TALK ABOUT SPIRIT.
WHEN WE SPEAK OF SPIRIT WE ARE NOT TALKING ABOUT A LOVED ONE IN THE AFTER-LIFE.

WE ARE TALKING ABOUT

1) THE SPIRIT THAT IS YOUR PERSONAL SPIRIT
2) THE SPIRIT THAT IS THE COLLECTIVE SPIRIT OF MANKIND
3) THE SPIRIT THAT IS IN THE AIR ALL AROUND US – THIS IS THE SPIRIT OF THAT WHICH WE CREATE COLLECTIVELY THROUGH OUR THOUGHTS, WORDS AND ACTIONS.

THIS FIRST SCENE OF THE PROPHECY EXPLAINS HOW MANKIND BEGAN IN SPIRIT AS A COMPLETE BEING – AS ADAM.
THEN IT EXPLAINS HOW THE SPIRITS OF ADAM AND EVE WERE THE FIRST BROKEN SPIRITS THAT EVENTUALLY EVOLVE INTO THE COLLECTIVE SPIRIT OF MANKIND.

THIS IS ALSO THE FIRST SCENE OF THE PROPHECY "THE REVELATION OF CHRIST" WHICH ILLUSTRATES ADAM AND EVE AS THE SON OF MAN WALKING AMONG SEVEN CANDLESTICKS AND SEVEN CHURCHES.

YOUR PERSONAL SPIRIT HAS SEVEN PARTS TO IT WHEN IT IS CONSCIDERED A BROKEN SPIRIT. AS YOUR SPIRIT HEALS, THESE SEVEN PARTS WILL BECOME ONE THEN YOUR SPIRIT AND SOUL FUNCTION AS ONE BEING IN LOVE AND LIGHT CONSCIOUSNESS.

THE COLLECTIVE SPIRIT OF MANKIND IS THE SUM TOTAL OF THE INDIVIDUAL SPIRITS OF ALL THE PEOPLE THAT ARE ALIVE TODAY.
THE COLLECTIVE SPIRIT HAS SUBSETS WITHIN IT THAT FUNCTIONS AS ONE. THOUSANDS OF YEARS AGO A COLLECTIVE SPIRIT WAS SEPARATED INTO THE SPIRIT OF A FAMILY, TRIBE AND NATION. ALL THE NATIONS OF THE WORLD MADE UP THE COLLECTIVE SPIRIT OF MANKIND. TODAY THIS REALITY IS CHANGING.

There are three chapters in the book of Genesis that have to be understood as three intricate parts of the reality of creation and our life in body, spirit and soul. In the third chapter Adam and Eve are clothed in skin. Being clothed in skin represents the moment in creation when the spirit and soul have a human experience. After they feed off the knowledge of good and evil (eat the apple from the tree of knowledge of good and evil) they have a human experience.

In the second chapter of Genesis life is breathed into the soul of Adam and he becomes a complete being. Adam is given the chance to exist in such a way as to have all of nature and creation to exist with. But it is not enough and Adam goes into a deep sleep. When the spirit and soul are asleep it ceases to exist and is basically dead to creation. The prophecy refers to this state of being as the spirit and soul having a name but is dead (you will learn more about this when you read chapter 2). After the spirit and soul go to sleep, Eve is created from the rib of Adam. This is the first time a broken spirit became a reality in nature and creation. In our lives today the complete separation of the spirit and soul occurs when our spirit is sealed into the emotionless reality of depression which the first scene of the prophecy refers to as the church of sloth.

In the first chapter of the book of Genesis man is created in God's image. This creation is the spirit of man. The collective spirit of man was and still is split into male and female halves. It was when Adam and Eve became a reality that the male and female were no longer one. They also represent the spirit and soul of creation. It is important to remember that these images and symbols tell several stories two of which are the history of the spirit and soul of mankind and how creation works throughout our lives.

The rest of the Bible chronicles the evolution of the body, spirit and soul; the journey into darkness and then the quest to find our light. Preserving this information was the original intention of the Bible's authors. The reason they needed to chronicle this reality is so we could reflect back on the trials and tribulations of our lives when the collective spirit was filled with darkness. The final book of the Bible contains a scene in it about the creation of a new city called the New Holy City of Jerusalem. This final scene represents the complete integration of the body, spirit and soul and all of its creations into pure consciousness. This is the end game for all of us. If there is an end of time this is it. After finding our Holy Grail (the oneness of our spirit) and then continuing to live a life and existence as a higher being of love and light we will achieve pure consciousness and no longer need a physical life form (a body) in order to exist of to just be.

As you will learn throughout this book the healing process requires that we reverse the effects of the events that caused us to live with a darker collective spirit.

The primary message of the prophecy and the parables is about forgiveness. It is about the need to create a forgiving spirit individually and collectively. There are groups of people (nations) that need to learn to forgive one another for the sins of the past. For example:

1) The Jewish race has learned to forgive those that nave persecuted them for many lifetimes.
2) Americans are learning to forgive Russians and others where a threatening environment existed in their lives.
3) People in Asia have to learn to forgive those that created a threatening of destructive reality in their lives.
4) Islam is learning to forgive Israel for the sins of the past that created hardships for their ancestors.
5) Religious and spiritual people have to learn to heal from the sins of the past that still plague our lives with anger and hatred that we project onto one another.

These are the lessons that this generation must learn to overcome.

Another message that comes from the prophecy is that we all must learn to agree. If we continue to dispute and argue about the things we disagree on we will continue to create the separation that has existed for thousands of years. When we realize the truths that we seek are hidden within each and every one of us we will learn to find ways to agree with each other. Then as we grow closer together the reality of living and loving will grow stronger within us as we no longer have a need to disagree but instead search for those areas in which we agree. Then we will learn the truths that have been hidden with in all of us for thousands of years.

IN THE BEGINNING (Creation and Evolution)

In the beginning God created creation. There was a purpose for all that was created. This original purpose was to create whatever was necessary to separate dark spirit from light spirit and to give the dark what it needed so it could transform its self from dark to light. The spirit of heaven and earth was created and there was darkness and then there was light. The dark and the light were separated by the firmament. The firmament also separated the physical from the spiritual (the waters above from the waters below). As the spirit of all that was created evolved into physical realities man was created so spirit can sense and feel it's-self; its own existence. Ultimately, creating the spirit and souls human experience is what creation created. Spirit cannot sense or feel its own existence; only through a human body can the body, spirit and soul experience the feelings and emotions that exist in our lives, this is what life is all about. Our experiences in life will determine the anger or love that is a reflection of our spirit at any moment in time.

In order to explain the realities of creation the book of Genesis was written. The seven days of creation explain several realities of creation:

1) the processes of creation that began – in the beginning
2) the sequence of events that existed when creation and evolution began
   a. this sequence of events
      i. created the spirit of that which was needed so creation could create
      ii. let the spirit of that which was created evolve
      iii. explain how creation and evolution made the physical reality that we now call life
3) The processes of creation through which we create all day long and every day of our lives. We create the spirit of our thoughts words and actions individually and collectively.

The spirit of man was created on the sixth day then in chapter 2 the soul of man evolved and in chapter 3 Adam and Eve (the first broken spirit) were clothed in skin and began the human experience. Chapter one created creation and all that is natural. Creation is the most natural reality of nature. Creation created all the elements of nature (earth, wind, fire and water) as well it created the spirit of the earth, seas, rivers and streams, sun, moon and stars and all the animals that inhabit the earth. The evolution of the spirit, soul into a physical reality is what is meant by the phrase, "God made". Creation and evolution allows all of this to exist. It is such an interactive system that even creation and evolution cannot exist without one another; this is what Genesis is explaining. Genesis is more than just the power of creation; it is about the power of genesis, the powers of creation and evolution that continue to exist in our lives as we evolve into all that we can be and will be. When I say we I mean all of life. The true power comes from the understanding that we are all one in nature, in creation and in evolution. We do not exist without the trees (spiritually as well as physically), we do not exist without the spirit of love that comes from life that is all around us (this life is in the trees, the air, the earth, animals etc....). The love and anger that exists in the spirit of nature only exists because mankind created it. Our anger, hatred and rage as well as love and compassion lives in us and in all of nature. You will gain a better understanding of this reality of life when you read the chapters in this book about the prophecy Revelations. It is the spirit of life that breathes life into the spirit and soul of each of us and we create the spirit of love and light (or darkness of anger) that exists in the air all around us. Yes, we create it and it feeds us all day long everyday life-time after life-time and generation after generation we created it, it feeds us and we feed it. This cycle of life is a very important reality of life that we all need to understand. We create the spirit of our thoughts words and actions. The spirit of our thoughts words and actions are made up of an intention or purpose and the emotions the combine with them to create the spirit of our creations. They exist in our spirits and in the air around us. They want to live and need us to feed them in order for them to live. The more we feel a feeling and then emit an emotion because of what we feel the more we feed that which we created.

AUTHORS COMMENT:

1) Please feel before you speak of act. Try to understand the feelings that are motivating your words and actions. When your words and actions are not accompanied by love and compassion resist acting on them. If you are upset please wait until your anger subsides and then respond in an appropriate way.
2) All things in creation have a spirit and consciousness. All things in creation are connected to one another through the spirit of everything.

THE HEAVEN AND THE EARTH

In the beginning God created Heaven and earth.
The earth was void. It had no emotion or consciousness; it was not committed to doing anything. It was empty.

As you read this book you will learn about the collective spirit of mankind and how the spirit of mankind exists in the kingdom of the heavens. Much like the earth exists in the universe the spirit of mankind exists in these heavens. The spirit of mankind is the spirit of the earth. In the beginning the earth was void because mankind had not yet created the spirit of its self. Over time we have created and re-created ourselves many times as we continue our quest through the emotions and consciousness of these heavens. Eventually we will create our collective light and find the peace and glory in which we seek.

DARKNESS WAS OVER THE DEEP AND GOD SAID LET THERE BE LIGHT

After the heavens and the earth were created there was darkness in the heavens but no light. The light evolves in the kingdom of the heavens as we live our lives and create it. The potential for light to exist was created but it is only potential until we are capable of creating it. This is symbolized in the prophecy as the first image in the second scene; this image is described as seven blazing lamps of fire sitting in front of a throne.

THE SPIRIT OF GOD WAS OVER THE WATERS

The waters separate the darkness from the kingdom of God (pure consciousness). The white light of spiritual existence that will exist after mankind has transformed its-self from dark to light to bright and then to God. The kingdom of the heavens is the bridge between the darkness of the deep and the kingdom of God.

THE LIGHT AND THE DARK

In the beginning there was only dark. Then God created the heavens and the earth and the let the light be. The dark was the spirit that needed to find its way back into the light. It was a quest that probably seemed unsurmountable. The angels worked to create that which was needed to help those dark and lonely souls find their way back into the light of day and then learn what is needed to evolve into an existence that was whole again.

The Bible is a journal that chronicles the life of mankind as our spirits and souls evolve through creation on our quest to re-create the spirit and soul that is our existence.
The Bible tells the story of the body, spirit and soul's journey into darkness and the quest to find our light again.
The Bible tells the story of creation and how it works through us to aide and guide us on our path home.

THE FIRMAMENT

In the air all around us is the spirit of that which we create; I call this the ambient spirit of mankind. With every thought, word and action we create the spirit of who we are at that moment in time, at that moment in creation. We cannot see or touch this ambient spirit but we can feel it; we can sense it and perceive its presence. Those that can sense it are said to have the spiritual gift of discernment of spirit. This ambient spirit that we can sense or feel is the emotion or thoughts that we feel from another person as we interact with him or her. This is what the firmament was created to do. It allows a place for our personal spirit to exist and a place for that which we create to exist. Our spirit exists as we live. The more we live, love and laugh the stronger our spirit thrives or the collective spirit thrives.

The firmament also separates the dark from the night. The dark and night are two parts of the kingdom of the heavens. When a person is on his journey into a darker reality he will naturally seal himself into this darker reality by creating a spirit that is not capable of holding light. When living with a spirit not capable of holding light he is has sealed his fate into this darker reality. The firmament now acts as a place for a person to learn how to love with a spirit that is not capable of holding light; it also acts as a place to teach us how to live in the light again.

THE KINGDOM OF THE HEAVENS

It is quite simple to understand what the kingdom of the heavens is. It is the source of all feeling and emotions, thoughts and consciousness. Consciousness is knowledge and awareness. The kingdom of the heavens is where the spirit and soul exists.

This is how it works. When someone has an intention to do something that is positive in nature she will feel the love of compassion of that intention. This positive feeling comes from the kingdom of the heavens, fills her spirit and motivates her to act. The thoughts that guide her actions also come from the kingdom of the heavens. These thoughts come through her soul's connection to the heavens and tell her to hug someone or to show her affection for what someone had done for her. A person that has an anger cased intention would receive a completely different feeling and a thought that is a reflection of those feelings.

In the heavens the light and dark of our creations exist as the emotion(s) of who we are. There is a light and dark of the heavens because there are positive (love-based) and negative (fear and anger-based) feelings and emotions in our lives. The firmament also separates the dark of night from the light of day. In the firmament is where the lesser light and the greater light exist.

If you visualize a barometer with three sections in it:

- The first section would be a black section at the bottom that represents the dark of night.
- A bright colored section at the top that represents the light of day.
- A gray section in the middle that represents the firmament that separates the dark from the light, you would have the kingdom of the heavens. The gray section is a place of transition for our emotions and consciousness. It would be seen as having two halves: The lower half would have a gray scale and the upper half a sort of gray scale mixed with colors. The prophecy, Revelations refers to this gray area of the firmament as a book with seven seals.

This barometer represents the full range of emotions and feelings as well as the full range of knowledge and consciousness that exists in the kingdom of the heavens. This range of emotions is what we are capable of feeling and living with. This gray area contains the lesser light and greater light of the heavens. The path to live in the bright light of the heavens will take a person's spirit through these two levels of light. After living in a darker reality we have to learn to live with light in our spirit and love in our heart again. These lesser and greater lights are there to help us learn to love again. This is where the collective spirit of mankind exists today.

FEAR – HEALTHY FEAR AND UNHEALTHY FEAR

To be filled with fear is to be afraid. To live with a spirit filled with fear is when a person becomes consumed by fear and begins this journey into a life filled with fear. To not be able to avoid a fearful event is when you feel terror. This is an unhealthy fear. Fear can also be part of a healthy reality in life. When you feel fear and then act in such a way as to avoid that something that caused the fear; you have a healthy fear. The best statement I have ever heard about fear comes from the movie "Coach Carter". It is about a high school basketball coach for an inner city school. Throughout the movie he repeatedly asks one of the high schools players, Timo Cruz, "What is your greatest fear?" Towards the end of the movie Timo answers with the following statement,

> "Our deepest fear is not that we are inadequate. Our deepest fear is that we are powerful beyond measure. It is our light, not our darkness, that most frightens us. Your playing small does not serve the world. There is nothing enlightened about shrinking so that other people won't feel insecure around you. We are all meant to shine as children do. It's not just in some of us; it is in everyone. And as we let our own lights shine, we unconsciously give other people permission to do the same. As we are liberated from our own fear, our presence automatically liberates others."

HOW OUR SPIRIT AND SOUL WORK TOGETHER TO CREATE FEELINGS AND THOUGHTS IN OUR DAY TO DAY LIVES

As we live our life we experience a specific range of emotions that we are capable of feeling and expressing. Each feeling we have fills our spirit with the light or dark of it and we are motivated to act on them. Then the thoughts and consciousness that are a reflection of these feelings will guide our actions. Our spirit allows us to feel feelings while our soul brings the thoughts and consciousness that guide our actions. This is how the body, spirit and soul work as one through our day to day lives as we create with every thought, word and action. This is why the kingdom of the heavens is so important. Without the creation of these heavens there would be no way for a darker spirit to experience its-self. When a person loses his or her ability to forgive he will create a seal that prevents the feelings and consciousness that exist in the light side of these heavens from entering his or her consciousness. This is why forgiveness is so important. When a person is very upset at someone else's actions and with a great deal of commitment says "I will never forgive you" or "I hate you" or some other phrase that carries the same meaning he creates a seal that stays in his spirit. This is how a person creates a seal. He will remain sealed away from love and light until he can forgive this other person with same strength of conviction that existed when the seal was created.

EVOLVING THROUGH THE LESSER LIGHT AND THE GREATER LIGHT OF THE HEAVENS

THE EMOTIONS AND FEELINGS OF THE LESSER LIGHT

This gray area that exists in our lives is created to allow a person (and all people collectively) to have a spirit that exists with either an expanding capacity to love (quest to create your light) or a diminishing capacity to love (journey into a darker reality). As we learn to love again we have to learn to forgive and then to love. This is a healing process that involves cleansing your spirit so you can feel deeper levels of caring, love and compassion again. Learning to feel again is the result of learning to create forgiveness in your spirit. As you experience life with feelings and emotions that previously did not exist in your life; they come from dealing with the emotions that were lost when you lived without them. To create through a deep rooted feeling of love and compassion is important; the challenge that many people faced thousands of years ago was that no light existed in the collective spirit of mankind. Two thousand or three thousand years ago, when people tried to deal with their issues in life they might have been able cleanse their spirit of the darkness that existed but could not create light in their personal spirits. There was no love or light in our lives or existence. It is a reality in creation that someone had to plant the seeds of love in order for mankind to be able to transform from dark to light. This is what Jesus brought into our lives. He lived with a forgiving and loving spirit and never lost his light. After being treated brutally and still loved those that wished to harm him and forgave them for their actions, he planted the seeds of love and forgiveness in the collective spirit of mankind.

MEMORIES AND CONSCIOUSNESS OF THE GREATER LIGHT

When a person is mistreated and is no longer able to forgive someone that hurts him a seal in his spirit is created. This seal prevents him from feeling any of the good feelings that existed before the seal was created. These feelings and memories are locked away and you are no longer allowed access to them. In the future any time you are in a situation in which you should express these feelings you will respond with either no feeling at all or have an anger based response. Even though a situation should require a different response; you are not capable of the positive response so you can only do the best you can with what you have.

In order to find these memories and feelings you have to search for them. You now have to earn your right to have them again. It is like you have to find the doors in your mind where these memories and feelings are sealed away and then find the keys to open these doors. Then the work begins to deal with the issues from your past so you can remove the seals that sealed your fate. The work you have to do is all about dealing with your issues in life and then forgiving those that hurt you or even wished you harm. You have to dig deep into your consciousness and spirit in order to reach the depth of your feelings and emotions in order to free your spirit of this seal that you created. You can do it and many people today are re-creating their spirits and souls.

As a person learns to live with a deeper state of emotional connection to life he or she will then evolve into the greater light of these heavens and gain a greater consciousness. As love-based consciousness grows in our spirit and soul we learn to live more in sync with our body, spirit and soul. It is this synchronicity that will bring a person's spiritual reality into the bright light of the heavens. This transition through the greater light of the heavens is the result of healing through the memories of the hardships that created our lives. After dealing with the emotional side of an issue it is only natural that we will have to deal with the memories associated with the experiences that created a weaker spirit. As we deal with the memories and learn to forgive more deeply we will release the seals that sealed our soul (consciousness). With a soul that is capable of sharing a deeper awareness of these realities that sealed our fate we will also become more aware of the reality of life around us. With this transformation of your spirit your perception of the world around us will change.

As your spirit evolves into this greater light your ability to sense and feel the world around you will expand. This will allow you to perceive the world and those in it in a very different way. This is what conscious awareness is all about.

SPIRITUAL AWARENESS OF THE BRIGHT LIGHT OF THE HEAVENS

The third leg of this quest to create a light-based reality occurs in the bright light of the heavens. This is the part of the heavens that Genesis refers to as the light of day. As a person releases the seals that existed in his life he grows a deeper emotional connection to life and a consciousness that accompanies these emotions. This emotion-based perception of life is the reality that will allow a person to release the seals that sealed his spirit in a darker place. As we grow into emotion-based consciousness the final part of the healing process will become a reality in his or her life. This part of the healing process heals the spirit and soul at its core. The key to maintaining your light is to grow into a life filled with emotion-based consciousness. To grow a spirit and soul that is light based you have to feel a feeling and then act on it in an appropriate way. You have to use your senses to feel your feelings and to better understand them; than act on the thoughts that are appropriate. While learning to sense and feel at this level you will learn that all the feelings that you feel are not necessarily what you might think of as yours. They could come from another person, a group of people, the collective spirit of mankind or the ambient spirit of mankind's creations. When you live without this sensitivity it is normal to believe that these feelings are your and therefore you should act on them. After all they come from within you; they come through your spirit. It is the source of these feelings that you will become more aware of. In the last 50 – 70 years mankind has entered this level of consciousness and refers to this reality as intuition. The Bible refers to it as the gift of discernment. Another gift that the Bible refers to is called the gift of knowledge; it is the gift of knowing that comes from gaining a greater conscious awareness. This gift is also very powerful because you can learn anything you want by just being committed to learning it. It may take a long time to get it but you can get it. If you seek a great truth you must have a purpose that is equally great in order to obtain the truth you seek.

Prior to a person experiencing hardships in his life, he lives with a spirit that is capable of being aware of the spirit around him. This awareness includes spiritual gifts like extrasensory perception and telepathy. Over time these senses make a person realize the hurtful intentions of others and it becomes difficult to continue to live with these sensing and feeling skills. As a person loses this high level of sensitivity he will only be able to rely on physical senses (seeing, hearing, smelling et al). When a person is evolving through the healing process that re-creates his spirit he will naturally regain this sensitivity to the environment around him. In order to regain this heightened sensitivity and awareness he or she will have to remember how it felt to lose this highest level of light because of the abusive nature of those that created the hurtful environment in the first place. The three dimensions of the healing process that rebuilds a person's spirit and soul include the following:

1) Emotional awareness - healing from emotional loss that completed the seals that sealed your fate. This dimension of the healing process heals the spirit.
2) Consciousness awareness - healing from the feelings, emotions and memories that were so hurtful in your past. This dimension of the healing process heals the soul.
3) Spiritual awareness - healing from the feelings, memories and conscious awareness that began your journey into the darker realities of life. This level of the healing process unites the spirit and soul as one being in love and light.

Each of these levels of the healing process brings with it a greater depth of emotion and the potential to achieve a greater consciousness in you and your life. As a person achieves a greater emotional connection to life he will gain a greater consciousness (connection to his soul). When a person achieves this higher level of spirituality, love-based consciousness becomes spirit-based consciousness. When a person's body, spirit and soul work in harmony with one another this spiritual healing is complete. At this level of healing you will live life with a greater awareness of the intentions of others as well as the dark and light of someone else's spirit. Learning to live with this heightened sensitivity is a big part of this healing process.

THE JOURNEY INTO DARKENSS

As a person journeys into a life without light in his spirit or love in his heart he will eventually reach a point in life when his journey will become a quest. This quest is about trying to find the love and light that was lost. On both the journey in dark and the quest to find light you will learn to exist in the lesser light and greater light of the firmament. While in the firmament you will learn to either live without light in your spirit or how to transform your dark spirit in to light. A journey into a darker state of mind begins when a person loses his or her ability to love. When a person's spirit loses its capability to hold light, it is only a matter of time until he or she can no longer forgive those that created an environment that did not nourish their spirit, with the love they needed. Fear then enters a person's life. As fear and anger consume a person's life their spirit loses the brightness that comes with a healthy spirit and soul as they enter this spiritual reality referred to as the greater light. As fear turns to anger and a person replaces the love that naturally made them feel good with increasing levels of anger, hatred and rage their weaker spirit becomes consumed by a darker grayness that is the lesser light of the firmament. Then when all the natural loves of life are lost this person has created the seals that seal their spirit into a darker state of mind (the abyss) and their spirit and soul now exists in the dark of night which is the abyss of creation.

The four loves that are lost while on this journey into darkness are:

1) Compassion - Love for those that wish you harm
2) Love of others especially family and close friends
3) Love of self
4) Love God, nature and creation

LIVING IN DARKNESS AND THE PRODIGAL SON MOMENT

People stay in this state of mind which is sealed away from the love and light of the heavens until they reach a moment in their life that gives them that something that they need to overcome the darkness of the spirit they created for themselves. The Bible refers to this moment in a parable that is commonly referred to as the, "Prodigal Son". The moral of this parable is that people will eventually get to a point in their life when they realize their spirit is not healthy as if they are sleeping with pigs. When they have an experience when this moment in time exists they will accept the reality that their actions are hurtful and not acceptable. Until this moment a person's mind rationalizes that the hurtful things you do to others is ok, as if the hurtful things you say or do are not really hurtful or that people deserve to be treated this way.

A darker or weaker spirit exists with other spirit that are of the same rhythm and vibration. These other spirits feed you the feelings and thoughts needed to motivate you to continue to live off them as they feed your spirit what you need to feel comfortable in your life. As you try to change and allow your spirit to evolve into a higher vibration it is the attraction that exists between you and this part of the collective spirit of mankind that strives to prevent your spiritual growth. The best analogy I can share with you is that it is similar to a bucket of crayfish. You never have to put a lid on a bucket of crayfish in order to keep them in the bucket. This is because if one of the crayfish tries to climb out of the bucket there will be others that will grab it and drag it back into the bucket. These crabs stay in the bucket until they become strong enough to overcome the strength of all the crabs that will try to prevent them from escaping.

At this moment in time a person accepts the depth of the reality of their life and has a deep desire to change it. The rationalization no longer has an effect on you. It is this deep desire to change that is critical to the process of creation that re-creates your spirit and soul. Without this commitment you will not be able to reach the depth of feeling needed to overcome the forces of nature that hold you in this darker reality. To re-create your spirit you have to want to change more than anything else in your life. You will want this change more than you will want anything that you ever had in your life; you will be willing to give up everything and everyone in your life for it. You will reach a point in time when you ill realize that you can make your life and the lives of others, better. This is when the quest to find light begins. This is your quest to find your Holy Grail. As you will learn through reading this book your spirit in light is your grail cup. When you have completed the process of healing your spirit and the seven parts that were broken become one and your body, spirit and soul function as one in body, spirit and soul you will have found your grail cup.

THE QUEST INTO LIGHT – RELEASING THE SEALS THAT SEALED YOUR FATE

After a person finds his commitment to re-creating his spirit he begins his quest to heal his spirit, find the light that will feed his spirit and the love he needs in his life. The quest is about reversing the negative nature of the spirit he has created. It is like reversing the polarity of a negative spirit by cleansing it of the darkness that has existed in it. Darkness exists in a person's spirit because a person has a spirit that is not capable of holding light.

The process of forgiveness cleanses the spirit of darkness by making it strong enough to hold light; thereby creating a reality in a person's life that will make him or her no longer want to hurt others. When this happens the spirit has emptied itself of its darkness and can now begin the process of learning to love again.

The first thing that happens to a spirit that becomes capable of holding light is you must first let it hold light. To allow your spirit to fill with light you have to act differently towards others than you did when your spirit was filled with fear and anger. It is natural to feel very motivated to not treat people in the way you had before cleansing your spirit. It is an overpowering feeling that will consume you. As you act in a caring manner your spirit will fill with the light of that caring reality that you created.

As your spirit fills with light you will feel the caring feelings that had left your life many years in the past. At first it is normal to feel uncomfortable to feel the feelings of caring, love mercy, compassion etc. Over time you will learn to let these feelings enter your life as you let yourself feel good about who you are and what you are doing in your life. As you feel good about your life you will feel comfortable sharing these positive feelings with others. At this point you are making a difference in the collective spirit of mankind. This is your contribution to making the world a better place.

As your emotions flow more smoothly from the light of your spirit through you and to others in your day to day life you are completing the process of re-creating your spirit. As you share the love you have created in your life with others you are co-creating a powerful spirit that will exist in the ambient spirit of mankind.

As you complete the process of Forgive and live with love you are able to leave the gray are of the firmament. This means that you have reversed your path and have gone back through the lesser light and greater lights of the firmament. Now you have to learn to maintain your light as you live and exist in the Light of Day.

THE HISTORY OF GOD'S VS GOD

An explanation of the Bible would not be complete without a discussion about God and why it makes so many different references to God. The Bible refers to God in many ways:

1) God (in the first chapter of the book of Genesis)
2) The Lord God (in the second chapter of the book of Genesis)
3) The God of Jacob and Isaac and Abraham
4) Revelations refers to The living God
5) Jesus refers to the God of the living and the God of the dead

This discussion would not be complete if it did not include the way many countries and nations referred to their many god's or deities in the past. Thousands of years ago there were:

1) Roman gods
2) Greek gods
3) Egyptian gods
4) Celtic gods
5) Germanic gods
6) Native American's had their gods
7) Alaskan's had theirs

In the beginning God created the heavens and the earth and God created man in his own image; God created the spirit of man (which is now referred to as the collective spirit of mankind). Then in the second chapter of creation the Lord God breathed life into the soul of man.

God the Creator created man and then the spirit of man evolved into the soul of Adam as a complete being was formed. The Lord God is the spirit of evolution that evolved from the creation of the kingdom of the heavens.

As Adam continued to evolve the first broken spirit created Eve. Now the male and female spirits and souls of Adam and Eve existed. The next step in this evolutionary process of creation was for mankind to evolve. Without the physical body the healing that was needed to re-create the broken spirit would not occur. The need for mankind is what led to its creation and evolution.

The spirit of mankind grew from generation to generation. The first generation was Cane and Abel. In this first generation Cain became jealous of Abel; then Cain kills Abel. This begins the creation of the spirit of envy that exists in the kingdom of the heavens. This is why the prophecy says that the church of envy is the beginning of God's creation. The prophecy has seven churches which are seven states of mind. These seven states of mind are wrath, greed, lust, gluttony, sloth, pride and envy.

Thousands of years later mankind had evolved and the collective spirit of mankind evolved also. People evolved into families and tribes and nations. In these families, tribes and nations existed a lot of fear and anger.

> Tribal leaders were told to do what the leader of the nation told them to do.
> Family leaders were told to do what the tribal leaders told them to do.
> Family members were told to do as the head of the family told them to do.

This grew into a very rigid structure where discipline was needed to ensure that everyone did as they were told and no one talked to members of rival nations. Since fear ruled their spirits it was like great walls separating nations from nations. It was like slightly smaller walls separated tribes from one another. Within families there was a similar feeling of having a wall between brothers and sisters.

This created the structure of the spirit of mankind. It was only natural that a tribe or nation that felt threatened would feel the collective fear and anger that existed within their collective spirit. When people felt vengeful they would say there God is a vengeful God, when there was a great amount of fear amongst a nation or tribe they might have said that there God is a fearful God or they might fear God.

God was the collective spirit of their tribe of nation. It was their fear or envy that they felt and this is what people used to refer to as God.

The Romans, Egyptians, Greeks and many others all created the spirit of the gods that existed within the spirit of their nation. When threatened by another nation or tribe, anger and rage would fill their spirits as the aggressive nature of their actions motivated them to go to war against an opposing tribe or nation. Hundreds of thousands of people acting on their aggression created the spirit of their aggression. This spiritual creation is much greater than that which a small group of people will create. Tis greater spirit is what used to be referred to as the God of war. The nation or tribe that could manifest the most aggression would be able to say that their god is greater than their opponent's god. When the wars were over the goddesses of love would then enter their collective spirit as the warriors would return home to those waiting for them to return. It is important to learn the power of the collective spirit of mankind to create the spirit of our thoughts, words and actions. When we all create with the same feelings and intentions we create a very powerful spirit that wants to live and exist in our lives. It wants to feed us and it wants to feed off of us.

So the God of Jacob and Isaac and Abraham refers to the collective spirit of the Israelites.

The Greek, Egyptian, Roman gods refer to the collective spirit of their thoughts, words and actions which is the spirit of their collective culture.

In the Book of Genesis God is in reference to the Creator that created creation and it explains how creations works through us.

In the book of Genesis the Lord God refers to the spirit of evolution that evolved from creation.

Then came the Roman Empire; it was responsible for 2,500,000 square miles of land mass and all the people and their beliefs in their god's. About 500 years after the Roman's invaded the Middle East they realized they had to create the spirit of the Roman Empire. They commissioned the Roman Catholic Church to integrate all the tribes and nations into one belief; into a belief in one God – the God of the Roman Empire. Through their efforts a meeting was held and all religious and spiritual leaders met to determine how to create this reality. These leaders were very spiritual and knew the truths about creation. Their challenge was that the Romans were intentionally suppressing the spirits of those within the empire. The people of the empire were only allowed to do what was necessary to feed the empire what it needed to survive. Their spirits were not free to express themselves. The leaders of the Roman Empire would never allow the truths that are entering our consciousness today to be taught to the people of their empire. If people knew these truths they would feel free to live outside of the constraints the Romans needed in place to maintain their control of the empire.

So the spiritual leaders that met to form the church and its teachings knew these truths about the creation and evolution of the spirit and soul. They also knew they could not let the Romans know these truths were in the Bible. So they hid these truths in the images and symbols of the prophecy, the parables of the New Testament and the story of Genesis.

The Bible's original intention was to preserve all the beliefs of the tribes and nations into one book that told two stories.

  1) the story of the evolution of man through the stories of the Israelites
  2) the story of the evolution of collective spirit and soul of mankind

Because it tells the story of the evolution of the collective spirit of mankind the Bible's Old Testament has many stories that are very destructive in nature. This is because the spirit of mankind at that point in time was destructive in nature. This was the beginning of God's creation.

Over time these spiritual leaders hoped to be able to teach these truths when the Roman Empire failed. The problem with this plan was that the empire did not fail until 800 years later and these truths were lost. After the fall of the empire the Roman Catholic Church was on its own and had to fend for its self. Now today the collective spirit of mankind has evolved to a point where these truths are entering our collective consciousness and we are learning about true spirituality nature's way. Nature's way is to evolve emotionally (spiritually) and then listen to our inner voice.

This takes us to the last three definitions of God:

1) The living God
2) The God of the dead
3) The God of the living

As the collective spirit of mankind continues to evolve we are collectively leaving the sense of being dead in spirit as our spirits come to life in the light side of the heavens. This will create the God of the Living. Today many people say their God is a loving God. This is because for the first time in our existence the collective spirit of mankind is learning to hold light so we can feel love.

The living God is the collective spirit of mankind. It creates the positive and negative realities that exist in all of us.

The God of the Living is that part of the collective spirit (living God) that is capable of holding light.

The God of the dead is that part of the collective spirit (living God) that is not capable of holding light.

Today many people are learning to accept that there is a creator that created and continues to create. The ancient teachers would have referred to the creator as God and that part of creation that continues to create as the Lord God. Today many people refer to creation and evolution as God.

Today we refer to the living god, god of the living and god of the dead as the collective spirit and collective consciousness of mankind. This is the collective spirit and soul of mankind.

CHAPTER 2

THE SON OF MAN WALKING AMONG 7 CANDLE STICKS

1. the son of man
2. the son of man walking among 7 candlesticks
3. the mystery of the 7 stars, 7 angels, 7 candlesticks and 7 churches
4. the 7 churches

THIS FIRST SCENE OF THE PROPHECY EXPLAINS THE EVOLUTION OF MANKIND INTO A DARKER REALITY – THE REALITY OF THE SEVEN CANDLE STICKS AND SEVEN CHURCHES.

THIS SCENE EXPLAINS HOW MANKIND'S CONSCIOUSNESS (THE COLLECTIVE SOUL) EXISTED WHILE WALKING AMONG SEVEN CANDLESTICKS AND THE REALITY OF OUR COLLECTIVE SPIRIT WHEN WE CREATED THIS DARKER REALITY IN OUR LIVES.

THE FIRST ACT OF CREATION BY MANKIND WAS WHEN ADAM AND EVE'S SON CAIN KILLED HIS BROTHER ABEL. IT WAS AN ACT MOTIVATED BY ENVY THROUGH WHICH CAIN CREATED THE SPIRIT OF HIS ACTIONS. HE ALSO BEGAN THE CREATION OF THE KINGDOM OF THE HEAVENS.

WE CREATE:

1) OUR OWN PERSONAL SPIRIT,
2) THE COLLECTIVE SPIRIT OF MANKIND,
3) THE AMBIENT SPIRIT THAT EXISTS IN THE AIR AROUND US.

HERE IS HOW CREATION WORKS TO CREATE THE KINGDOM OF THE HEAVENS - AS WE CREATE THE REALITY THAT IS THESE THREE SPIRITS; WE CREATE THEM IN THE KINGDOM OF THE HEAVENS AS WE CREATE THE KINGDOM OF THE HEAVENS.

ANOTHER WAY OF SAYING THIS IS – AS WE EXPERIENCE LIFE WITH DEEP SEEDED EMOTIONS WE CREATE THESE EMOTIONS FOR OTHERS TO EXPERIENCE THEM ALSO. SOMEONE MUST EXPERIENCE DEEP SEEDED EMOTIONS AND CREATE THROUGH THEM; THIS CREATES THE SPIRIT OF THEIR EMOTIONS. WHEN THE SPIRIT OF THESE EMOTIONS EXISTS IN THE AIR AROUND US IT WILL MOTIVATE OTHERS TO EXPERIENCE THEM TOO.

THIS WORKS FOR ANGER AS WELL AS LOVE.

IN THE BEGINNING WE CREATED WRATH AND HAVE SPENT OUR ENTIRE EXISTENCE LEARNING TO TRANSFORM IT INTO LOVE.

THE BIBLE AND THIS PROPHECY CHRONICLES THIS CREATION THROUGHOUT TIME.

THE SON OF MAN

The Son of Man represents several realities related to the story of the evolution of the body, spirit and soul of mankind.

Firstly, it is the complete being that evolved from the spirit of man which was created on the 6th day of Genesis. When the Lord God breathed life into the soul of man and a complete being was formed the spirit and soul of Adam was the complete being that is the Son of Man. As Adam dis-evolved into Adam and Eve (the first broken spirit) the Son of Man became the collective soul of Adam and the seven churches Eve) the collective spirit of mankind). Today the Son of Man and seven churches represent the spirits and souls of all of the people that live on the earth today and all that will incarnate (or reincarnate) into a life in the future (the collective spirit and collective consciousness).

Many times throughout the parables of the Bible's New Testament there are references to the Son of Man and the Son of God. There are four books of the New Testament called the books of Matthew, Mark, Luke and John. They present stories called parables. These stories explain how the individual and collective body, spirit and soul work through the kingdom of the heavens. The books of Matthew, Mark and Luck emphasize life in the kingdom of the heavens and the book of John emphasizes life in the kingdom of God. When these books begin talking about the body, spirit and soul the first thing they talk about is the Son of Man and then talk about the broken spirit. Below is an example of how the Bible explains the son of man and the broken spirit:

THE SON OF MAN

> *"And a scribe came and said to him: Teacher, I will follow thee wherever thou goest. And Jesus said to him: The foxes have dens, and the birds of the heaven have roosts, but the Son of man has not where he may lay his head."* (Matthew 8.19 – 8.20)

THE BROKEN SPIRIT

> *"And Jesus said to them: Can the sons of the bride chamber mourn while the bride groom is with them? But days will come when the bridegroom shall be taken away from them, and then will they fast. No one puts a piece of unfulled cloth on an old garment; for that which fills it up takes from the garment, and a worse rent is made. Neither do they put new wine into old bottles; otherwise, the bottles break, and the wine runs out, and the bottles perish; but they put new wine into new bottles, and both are preserved together."* (Matthew 9.15 – 9.17)

When Jesus refers to the son of man as having nowhere to lay his head he is referring to the fact that the son of man is a spiritual reality. The son of man has nowhere to rest its head because the spirit and soul never sleeps.

The statement about the bride groom will be taken away from the brides chamber is referring to the spirit and soul of mankind leaving the light side of the heavens. This occurs as the reality of a broken spirit exists in our lives. Just like an old garment cannot be repaired by simply sewing a new patch on it, a broken spirit also cannot be mended with a patch. It has to be taken apart completely and recreated. When the spirit is whole again it will be stronger and capable of holding the light that it lost when we were faced with hardships and suffering. Just like a new bottle of wine is needed to hold fresh wine a re-born spirit will hold a brighter light.

In the book of Genesis, when Adam goes from being a complete spirit and soul to being Adam and Eve this is the first broken spirit. This is the same as the bride groom leaving the brides chamber.

THE SON OF MAN AND SEVEN CANDLESTICKS

Walking among seven candlesticks tells the story of the spirit and soul in the beginning as existing in the darkness that the book of Genesis refers to as the deep. The book of Genesis says that darkness was over the deep while the vision, "Revelations" uses the symbol of seven candlesticks. They are candlesticks because they represent our potential to hold light but since the candlesticks are not lit they represent the darkness of the beginning of our existence.

Thus far the prophecy has told the story of the beginning of the spirit and soul as one being and then its journey into the darkness that existed within its-self. Soon you will learn about how the broken spirit and soul are illustrated in the prophecy.

THE MYSTERY OF THE SEVEN STARS, 7 ANGELS, SEVEN CANDLESTICKS AND 7 CHURCHES

The first riddle of the prophecy is,

> *"The mystery of the seven stars that thou sawest in my right hand, and the seven golden candlesticks. The seven stars and angels of the seven churches, and the seven candle sticks are seven churches"* (REV. 1:20).

The prophecy describes of the Son of Man thru twelve symbols. One of the symbols describes seven stars that are in his right hand. The last image in this first scene describes seven churches; each has an angel in it. This riddle states that the seven stars and the angels of the seven churches and the seven candle sticks are the seven churches.

The seven churches describe the seven parts of the broken spirit (collective spirit) that is mankind. Altogether these seven churches are the collective spirit of mankind. Individually they are the parts of mine and your broken spirit that will heal over time. As they heal they will integrate into one spirit that would then be an angel. This journey or quest that is our lives is all about healing the broken spirit of an angel.

The seven angels of the seven churches are the seven parts of our spirit. This is how the prophecy represents a broken spirit. An angel is a spirit that is pure in intention. To best describe spirit is to describe its three components; intention (or purpose), emotion and polarity. These three components combine to create the spirit of our creations. The angel represents one of these components; that component is the intention or purpose that is committed to the spirit of that which we create through our thoughts, words and actions. The candle sticks represent the darker or negative polarity and the stars represent emotions. The church is what houses the spirit of wrath, greed, lust, gluttony, sloth, pride and envy. As the prophecy continues the angels leave the churches and are seen with trumpets and cups. As the angels leave these darker states of mind they evolve into what they will be. Throughout mankind's history they first created a darker reality because they lost the light that existed within it. Then they existed in a state of mind that was filled with plagues. When filled with plagues we realized there had to be a better way and have started our collective quest to find our light. As time goes on we will continue to evolve our collective spirit into a greater consciousness. This greater consciousness becomes the collective consciousness in light as we create the light side of the kingdom of the heavens. The seven parts of the light side of the heavens will be the polar opposite spirit of wrath, greed, lust, gluttony, sloth, pride and envy. The challenge to understanding the prophecy is that these images and symbols describe mankind's journey up to the point in time when Jesus lived on the earth but it also includes and explanation our quest to create the light side of the heavens how to grow beyond these heavens.

AUTHORS COMMENT:

I do not want anyone reading this to take the prophecies statement about the angels leaving the churches to mean that we need to stop going to church on Sunday in order to evolve spiritually. As a matter of fact, today, we need these traditional churches to help us to learn how to experience life with a greater light in our spirit and consciousness from our soul.

The seven stars seen in the right had of the Son of Man are also mentioned in the first sentence that describes the first church and the firth church. These seven stars in this first church represent the time when the collective spirit and soul lost its positive emotions. When they are mentioned in the fifth church the statement includes a reference to the seven spirits of God and the seven stars. This is because we are on our quest to create the light side of the heavens. In the beginning there were only the darker emotions and when mankind had collectively created through the darkness of these heavens and are now learning to find our light we will be seen with the seven spirits of God. The seven spirits of God are the positive emotions through which we will explore, experience and create the light side of the heavens. It is important to remember that when we are on the light side of the heavens it does not mean that we leave the darker realities behind. It does mean that we have expanded our creating in the heavens and now can experience both light and dark feelings and emotions. This is where choice in our lives becomes a reality. We have to be sensitive enough to recognize where anger based feelings come from and then choose to create through anger or to wait until the anger leaves and then create through love based feelings.

These positive emotions will exist in our spirit as the collective spirit of mankind evolves into a healthier and stronger spiritual reality. A healthier and stronger spirit will allow the soul to exist in the light side of the heavens.

Candlesticks represent the darker side of the heavens while blazing lamps of fire (which are introduced into the prophecy as the first image of the second scene) represent the lighter side of the heavens. This is the positive or negative realities that exist in our spirit. Another way to explain this positive or negative reality is to say that there is a positive or negative polarity that exists in our spirit. Candlesticks and blazing lamps of fire represent the negative and positive polarity or our spirit. In this part of the prophecy it is the negative polarity that existed in the beginning.

The seven candlesticks represent the darker parts of the kingdom of the heavens in which the soul of mankind exists when the spirit of mankind is at its darkest point in its existence. The riddle says that all three of these come together to make the spirit of mankind when it was not capable of holding light; when it was consumed by darkness.

Therefore these seven churches house the spirit of mankind. The spirit of mankind has three components:

1) the purpose or that which it is committed to (angels)
2) the light or dark of the spirit; its polarity (blazing lamps of fire or candlesticks)
3) the emotion that is committed to the spirit of that which mankind was in the beginning (stars)

The prophecy describes each of the seven churches. They are the spirit of the seven deadly sins. In the beginning the spirit of man was filled with the essence of wrath, greed, lust, gluttony, sloth, pride and envy. These seven churches are seven states of mind that house the spirits (angel) of these seven deadly sins. Each of these churches has seven levels of the spirit that is the church. For example there are seven levels of fear and anger that leads up to the feeling of wrath. This church of wrath begins with fear that grows into anger, hatred, rage, ire, distain and then wrath. The church of sloth begins with depression and then grows into the deepest depression which is sloth. Each of these churches represents a spirit that exists in a negative way. The best way to describe this negativity of spirit is to think of it as having a polarity that is negative or the opposite rhythm and vibration of a positive spirit. This is why many people dance to the beat of a different drum. When your spirit has a vibration and rhythm you will feel more comfortable around certain music because it gives you a beat (rhythm and vibration) that makes you feel good.

PLEASE REMEMBER:

When the prophecy refers to a spirits intention it is not saying that we should have a deliberate intention to do something or to manifest something into our lives. It is saying that our spirit and soul exists with a potential to create with a darkness or light that is a function of who we are at any moment in time. We will create through the depth of emotion that we are capable of experiencing at any moment in time. As you will learn until a person creates a forgiving spirit he or she is not capable of living in light or expressing a deep love through his or her spirit. It is what comes through us naturally not what we want everyone to think we are but who we actually are that will create the reality that is our life.

REPENT AND OVERCOME – FORGIVE AND LIVE WITH LOVE

There are two parables that explain how the forgiveness and living with love are process of creation. They are processes that recreate our spirits so they are capable of holding light so we can feel love. Jesus talks about these processes in the following:

"Then came Peter and said to him: Lord, how often shall my brother sin against me and I forgive him? Till seven times? Jesus says to him: I say not to thee, till seven times, but till seventy times seven. For this reason the kingdom of the heavens is likened to a man, a king, who wished to take up a settlement with his servants. And when he had begun to settle, there was brought to him one that owed him ten thousand talents. And as he was not able to pay, the lord commanded him to be sold, and his wife, and his children, and all that he had, and payment to be made. Falling down therefore, that servant worshipped him, saying: Have patience with me, and I will pay thee all. And the lord of that servant moved with pity loosed him, and forgave him the debt. But that servant went out and found one of his fellow servants that owed him a hundred denarii; and laying hold on him he took him by the throat, saying: Pay, if thou owest any thing. Falling down therefore, his fellow servant besought him, saying: Have patience with me, and I will pay thee. But he would not; but went and threw him into prison till he should pay the debt. Therefore his fellow servants seeing what had been done, were greatly grieved, and came and made known to their lord all that had been done. Then his lord called him and said to him: Wicked servant, all that debt I forgave thee, because thou didst entreat me: did it not behoove thee also to have mercy on thy fellow servant, as I also had mercy on thee? And being angry his lord delivered him to the tormentors, till he should pay all that was due him. So also will my heavenly Father do to you, if you from your hearts forgive not each one his brother." (Matthew 18:21 – 18:35)

When Jesus said you have to forgive 70 times 7 times he was referring to a kingdom of the heavens. The 70 refers to the 7 churches and the 7 refers to 7 levels within each church. When a person or the collective spirit of mankind begins its quest to find light it is only natural that we will seek to create forgiveness in our spirit. When we begin in the darkest of the seven churches (envy) we will have to grow past the issues that created envy in our lives. We will then grow past the mountain of issues related to each of these seven churches. As we deal with the issues related to each of these churches we will have to seek forgiveness at each of the seven levels that exist in each church. This is why Jesus said we have to forgive 70 times 7 times. When we have completed this process of forgiveness we will have created a forgiving spirit. The most important part of this parable is that you have to forgive from your heart. When you try to create forgiveness in your spirit you hate to mean it you have to commit as much love as possible to what you are doing. Whether creating forgiveness, mercy, acceptance, faith etc.

Another important reality of creation is about using love to create a forgiving spirit.

> *"And Jesus answered and said to him: Simon, I have something to say to thee. He replied: Teacher, say on. A certain creditor had two debtors: the one owed him five hundred denarii, the other, fifty. As they had nothing to pay, he forgave them both. Which of them then would love him the more? Simon answered and said: I suppose that he to whom he forgave the more. He said to him: Thou hast rightly judged.*

> *And turning to the woman, he said to Simon: Seest thou this woman? I entered thy house; water for my feet thou gavest not; but she with her tears has moistened my feet, and with her hair has wiped them. A kiss thou gavest me not; but she from the time I came in has not ceased to kiss my feet. With oil my head thou didst not anoint; but she with ointment has anointed my feet. Wherefore, I say to thee, her sins which are many are forgiven, because she loved much; but he to whom little is forgiven, loves little. And he said to her: Thy sins are forgiven."* (Luke 7:40 – 7:48)

Another important statement made by Jesus is, "if you love a little you will be forgiven a little and if you love a lot you will be forgiven a lot". In this statement he is saying that if you want to create a forgiving spirit you have to create it with love. This means, you have to infuse love in the forgiveness that you seek. You create forgiveness by having an intention to forgive or be forgiven, you have to mean it and commit as much love as you can into this commitment. The forgiveness you create in your spirit is a function of how much love you commit to it. In the beginning when a person starts this process of forgiveness he or she may not have a lot of love to commit to it and that is OK. You might have to create a little forgiveness and then receive a little love and then use that love to create more forgiveness. You might have to do this many times as you go through the process of forgiveness and learning to love again.

Another statement made by Jesus is that the Son of Man will forgive you. This statement relates to the reality that his life created in the collective spirit of mankind. When he lived to forgive and love he planted the seeds that created forgiveness and love in the collective spirit of mankind (the Son of Man); therefore he made it possible for individual people to now create forgiveness and love in their personal spirits. Someone had to create it in the collective spirit before others could experience it. This is how he solved the problem that plagued mankind and our collective spirit since the days of Moses. As we continue to create more love and forgiveness the seeds he planted continue to grow.

THE SEVEN CHURCHES

In the beginning God created the playing field which is called the kingdom of the heavens. Then mankind created the seven churches. The seven churches are seven states of mind in which our spirit and soul exist. This is where the healing of our spirits starts. As we live and exist in the darkness of these seven churches we will create a desire to change and this will motivate us to grow into a better place in our lives.

During his lifetime St. John had started seven churches. The prophecy was seen by St. John. It is normal for a dream, vision or prophecy to appear to someone and use reference points that are familiar to that person to explain its message. The prophecy refers to these seven churches as:

1) Ephesus (the spirit of wrath)
2) Smyrna (the spirit of greed)
3) Pergamus (the spirit of lust)
4) Thyatira (the spirit of gluttony)
5) Sardis (the spirit of sloth)
6) Philadelphia (the spirit of pride)
7) Laodicea (The spirit of envy)

The prophecy begins by describing the 12 parts of the son of man and the spirit of each of its churches. Each church begins with a statement that links the Son of Man to the church. This linking is to show the part of the soul that connects to the spirit, as the broken spirit evolves into a stronger healthier being the spirit and soul will reconnect or rebuild its-self. In the last scene of the prophecy (the New Holy City of Jerusalem) the healing of the spirit and soul becomes complete as these characteristics of the spirit and soul are mentioned again.

Also, throughout the descriptions of the churches there is a statement in each that defines its spirit as one of the seven deadly sins.

The spirit of the states of mind that are the churches explain them-selves to the reader as the prophecy explains a broken spirit.

EPHESUS (THE SPIRIT OF WRATH)

The phrase that describes this church as the church of wrath is, *"But this thou hast, that thou hatest the works of the Nicolaitans, which I also hate."* (Rev. 2:6)

The prophecy is describing how a person feels as he or she loses their first love (compassion for those that wish you harm). In this state of mind a person has to work hard to hold on to the light in his or her spirit. In this state of mind we work hard to be patient with others because it is longer a natural feeling to just accept others for who they are. It becomes hard to endure the hardships that are created by others as you are losing your light. Eventually, when others that do the best they can with what they have, but still fail to create an environment that will nourish your spirit will create an unforgiving reality in your life. People that do the best they can with what they have but cannot nourish your spirit with what it needs, will think of them-selves as being as righteous as apostles but are not. This reality will begin to transform your spirit, your feelings and thoughts. Your spirit (feelings and thoughts) will guide you to believe that these people that you once trusted are now liars. This is when you begin to hate those that have fooled or tricked you into losing your light. This perception replaces the truths that used to fill your life.

The following is a quote from the prophecy that describes this first church of Ephesus:

> *"To the angel of the church in Ephesus write: These things says he that holds the seven stars in his right hand, that walks in the midst of the seven golden candlesticks; I know thy works, and thy labor, and thy patience, and that thou canst not endure evil men, and hast tried those that say that they are apostles and are not, and hast found them liars; and thou hast patience, and hast endured because of my name, and hast not fainted. But I have against thee that thou hast left thy first love.*
>
> *Remember therefore whence thou hast fallen, and repent and do the first works: else, I am coming to thee, and will move thy candlestick out of its place, unless thou repent. But this thou hast, that thou hatest the works of the Nicolaitans, which I also hate.*
>
> *He that has an ear, let him hear what the Spirit says to the churches: To him that overcomes will I give to eat of the tree of life, which is in the paradise of my God."* (Rev. 2:1 – 2: 7)

SMYRNA (THE SPIRIT OF GREED)

The phrase that describes this church as the church of greed is,

> *"I know thy affliction and thy poverty, (but thou art rich) and the blasphemy of those that say that they are Jews and are not, but are a synagogue of Satan"* (Rev. 2.9)

The essence of the spirit of greed is that you feel like you are poor and needy while actually you have enough or more than enough to survive. It is this feeling that motivates you to act in such a way as to want to acquire more of what you already have enough of. The reason a person feels this way is because they lost their first love (compassion) and now their second love (love of others especially family and close friends). Without these loves to naturally make you feel good about your-self and your life you replace the love in your life with fear and anger. You learn to use things to replace the love you used to feel for those that are now creating the emotional pain that exists in your life.

When people experience life in this greed based state of mind they are creating through fear and anger-based wants and needs. Wants and needs are the essence of the spirit of greed. As you will learn throughout this book, desires are the essence of lust and cravings are the essence of gluttony. When we feel, needy we use things to replace the loves we lost. When greed no longer makes you feel good about yourself, desires grow within your spirit. A desire to use people to do something for you to make you feel good about yourself replaces love of self. The need to use people and to have things in your life combine at a higher level as you learn to crave both as you create the spirit of gluttony in your personal spirit. This is how we create the spirit of greed, lust or gluttony in our lives. It is also how we created these churches in the kingdom of the heavens.

> As fear enters our life we lose our compassion and enter the church of Ephesus (wrath).
> As greed feeds our anger we live with a spirit consumed by the anger of the church of Smerna.
> As lust fills our spirit we feed off the desires and hatred of the church of Pergamus.
> As gluttony fills our spirit we feed off the cravings and rage of the church of Thyatira.

As you read the quote from the prophecy that is listed below you will see there is a link between the fear and anger as well as the feeling of being lied to (the first church) and the stronger negative blasphemous feelings of those that mislead you. It is these feelings that are taking your spirit into a darker place than just feeling fear and anger. As a person acts on their fear and anger they will create the darkness of that fear and anger in their spirit. This is what happens as a person goes from the first church into the second. You should be able to see how the fear and anger of the first church are linked to each other and are the feelings that feed this second state of mind (greed). Greed is fed by anger. The anger of wrath is the foundation of each of the churches. Wrath interacts with each of the churches as fear grows into anger and then hatred, rage, ire, distain and wrath.

One of the things Jesus said about greed came from a person that wanted to be like him. He told Jesus he had done everything that Jesus had been teaching and asked what else he had to do in order to follow him on his quest. Jesus knew he was a wealthy man and told him to give away all of his things and then he could walk his path with Jesus. Jesus was not saying that everyone has to be poor in order to be rich in spirit. He was telling this person that he must give away his things because the spirit of his purchases was greed based. When we purchase something the mere act of the purchase creates the spirit of the purchase. When the wants and need of greed are the essence of the purchase we create the foundation of greed in our spirit. To re-creates this reality in your life is to give away all the things you had; this act of generosity cleanses your spirit of the greed so you can then re-create it. You re-create your spirit without greed when you are generous in giving for what you receive and are grateful for what you have. When you are truly grateful for what you have and when you make a purchase you are generous in giving for what you purchase you will change the polarity of the greed based spirit you once had. This is the moral of the story.

The following is a quote from the prophecy that describes this second church of Smyrna:

> *"And to the angel of the church in Smyrna write: These things says the First and the Last, who was dead and revived; I know thy affliction and thy poverty, (but thou art rich) and the blasphemy of those that say that they are Jews and are not, but are a synagogue of Satan. Fear in no way the things that thou art about to suffer. Behold now, the devil is about to cast some of you into prison that you may be tried, and you shall have affliction ten days. Be thou faithful to death, and I will give thee the crown of life.*
> *He that has an ear, let him hear what the Spirit says to the churches: He that overcomes shall not be hurt by the second death."* (Rev. 2.8 – 2.11)

PERGAMUS (THE SPIRIT OF LUST)

The phrase that describes this church as the church of lust is,

> *"But I have against thee a few things: thou hast there those that hold the teaching of Balaam, who taught Balak to put a stumbling-block before the sons of Israel and to cause them to eat idol-sacrifices and to commit lewdness."* (Rev 2:14)

As a person lives with a weakened spirit his wants and needs motivate him to get what he wants and needs to make him happy. Most people will do whatever it takes to feel good again even if it means causing suffering in others. A person that hurts others will create an even weaker spirit for himself. This leads him down an even darker path as he loses his love of self.

Here you can see that greed grows into lust as a person learns to feed off of things (eating idol sacrifices; greed) and committing lewdness (lust).

As a person loses his love of self his spirit becomes weaker and is less capable of holding light. This creates a void in his spirit that leaves him with a feeling of emptiness that can only be filled by healing his spirit; by forgiving himself for all the hurt he caused others. Most people do not have that something we need to face the truths related to how we hurt others, so we continue down this path of darkness. This void in our spirit becomes a strong force in our lives as it forces us to act in ways that make us feel good even if it means we have to treat others very poorly in order to feel good. The more we do to hurt others the more we need things or someone to tell us we are OK. It is like when someone goes along with the rest of a crowd that is judging someone or mistreating someone; the feeling of being accepted by this group of others feels better than begin rejected by them. Rejection can be a very powerful motivator used by someone that manipulates others.

When a person uses others so he can feel good about himself, he is using others so he can deny what he did in the past to others was wrong. Every time a person hurts someone else he hurts his spirit. The more a person has to use others to feel good the more pain and hurt his spirit feels. In order to live in this hurtful state of spirit people rationalize that the hurtful things they do to others is either justified or that it really is not all that bad. To rationalize that I feel very bad so the hurtful things I am doing to you is not as bad as it could be is a way that people justify their actions. If a person had the sensitivity that comes with love he or she would never be able to mistreat others. What a shame that we have to take this journey in order to appreciate what we have. As a person experiences these lower vibrating realities his or her spirit is changing its polarity. As this polarity changes you are losing your connection to the love and light of the heavens and learning how live with a spirit not capable of holding light.

In this third church of lust we are ruled by our desires. Desires motivate us to use others to get what we want. In this state of mind it is not enough to have what we want but we feel better when we can use others to get what we want. Deceptive and manipulative behaviors are the primary characteristics of the desires of this lustful state of mind. Over time it is not enough to use people to get the things we want or need as physical needs replace the need to have things in our life. This more traditional understanding of lust still has its essence in a desire to use someone so we can feel better about our-self.

To be manipulative or deceptive is to say one thing but to use your words to try to get what you want. It is like you are talking out of both sides of your mouth or as if you have a double edged sword coming out of your mouth. In this state of mind you are trying to use your words to get what you want instead of being sincere with others you learn to make people think you are being sincere while actually misleading them. As people become highly skilled at this reality in their life they always find ways to prevent people from learning the truths about their manipulations and deceptions.

The following is a quote from the prophecy that describes this third church of Pergamus:

"And; to the angel of the church in Pergamus write: These things says he that has the sword two-edged, sharp I know where thou dwellest, where the throne of Satan is; and yet thou boldest fast my name, and didst not deny my faith, even in the days in which Antipas was my faithful witness, who was slain among you, where Satan dwells.

But I have against thee a few things: thou hast there those that hold the teaching of Balaam, who taught Balak to put a stumbling-block before the sons of Israel and to cause them to eat idol-sacrifices and to commit lewdness. So hast thou also in like manner those that hold the teaching of the Nicolaitans. Repent therefore; otherwise I am coming to thee quickly, and I will war against them with the sword of my mouth.

He that has an ear, let him hear what the Spirit says to the churches: To him that overcomes I will give of the hidden manna; and I will give him a white stone, and on the stone a new name written, which no one knows but he that receives it." (Rev. 2.12 – 2.17)

When the prophecy refers to worshipping or sacrificing idols it is about needing things (greed).

THYATIRA (THE SPIRIT OF GLUTTONY)

The phrase that describes this church as the church of gluttony is,

"But I have against thee that thou sufferest thy wife Jezebel, who says that she is a prophetess, and teaches and leads my servants astray to commit lewdness and to eat idol-sacrifices, And I gave her time to repent, and she will not repent of her lewdness. Behold, I cast her into a bed, and those that commit adultery with her into great affliction, unless they repent of her works. And her children will I kill with death; and all the churches shall know that I am he that searches the reins and the hearts; and I will give to you, to each one, according to your works." (Rev. 2.20 – 2.23).

The spirit of gluttony is a combination of both greed and lust. A gluttonous spirit is more consuming in nature; it is all consuming. When a person loses his or her love of all that is natural this spirit of gluttony begins to consume them. To lose your love of God, Nature and Creation is to no longer have any connection to the love and light side of the heavens. Another way to phrase this reality is to say that you are sealed away from the light of the heavens. This is when your spirit can no longer access the knowledge and consciousness that comes with a love based spirit. You will learn more about the significance of this phrase as you read the next chapter of this book.

Gluttonous realities create a life that is often consumed by overdoing things in life. To overdo things is to work so hard at trying to do what you think is the right thing to do that you believe you are doing what is right; but actually you are only trying to suppress or control the bad feelings that exist in your life. When you can no longer suppress or deny these feelings you will slip into the abyss as you learn to live with and accept your spirit as it is. This is when the polarity of your spirit is almost completely reversed. You now live with a spirit only capable of anger-based consciousness. Your spirit and love-based soul are completely separated and your only consciousness comes from the abyss of the dark side of the kingdom of the heavens.

People stay in this abyss until they have their prodigal son moment and then begin their quest into the light of day.

The following is a quote from the prophecy that describes this fourth church of Thyatira:

"And to the angel of the church in Thyatira write: These things says the Son of God, who has his eyes as a flame of fire, and his feet like burnished brass: I know thy works and thy love and thy faith and thy service and thy patience, and thy works the last more than the first. But I have against thee that thou sufferest thy wife Jezebel, who says that she is a prophetess, and teaches and leads my servants astray to commit lewdness and to eat idol-sacrifices, And I gave her time to repent, and she will not repent of her lewdness. Behold, I cast her into a bed, and those that commit adultery with her into great affliction, unless they repent of her works. And her children will I kill with death; and all the churches shall know that I am he that searches the reins and the hearts; and I will give to you, to each one, according to your works.

But to you I say, to the rest that are in Thyatira, as many as have not this teaching, such as have not known the depths of Satan, as they say, I lay upon you no other burden; but what you have hold fast till I come. And he that overcomes and that keeps my works to the end, to him will I give authority over the nations, and he shall rule them with a rod of iron, as the vessels of a potter shall they be broken to pieces, as I have received from my Father, and I will give him the morning star.

He that has an ear, let him hear what the Spirit says to the churches." (Rev. 2.18 – 2.29)

There is a pattern in the prophecy that is important to remember. This pattern relates to the first four of the seven parts of the spirit and the last three parts of the spirit. The first four parts of the spirit are all about the emotions of the spirit. The last three parts of the spirit link the spirit to the soul. As you read this book you will learn about love-based consciousness and anger-based consciousness. Emotion based consciousness is one of the keys to life and to how we create the reality that is our life. As the first four parts of our spirit (these exist outside of our bodies) fill with an emotion we will be motivated to act on them. Our soul will then guide our thoughts as we act on these feelings and thoughts.

AUTHORS COMMENT:

These first four churches all refer to the loves that are lost. They talk about how we either live with love in our lives thereby naturally feeling good about our life; or live in a state of mind where love is replaced with fear, anger, hatred and rage. With a spirit filled with anger, hatred and rage we strive to use people and things to replace the good feelings we used to have when we lived with love in our hearts.

These next three churches are a little tricky to interpret because they have to explain two realities. One reality relates to experiencing life in the pit of the abyss and the other is the polar opposite. Both realities are explained in the message of the churches of sloth, pride and envy.

SARDIS (THE SPIRIT OF SLOTH)

The phrase that describes this church as the church of sloth, *"I know thy works, that thou hast a name that thou livest, and art dead."* (Rev. 3.1)

This state of mind is the first step a person takes when their spirit exists in the abyss of his or her spiritual reality. Sloth is a spiritual reality that is defined as being dead to creation. To have a name but to be dead is to live with a spirit that is so depressed that it has no rhythm or vibration. With no rhythm or vibration this spirit has no power to create at all. As a person's spirit continues its journey into a darker state of mind he or she will be motivated to live through pride. It is through pride that a person learns to create a spirit that is out of phase with the rhythm and vibration of a positive spirit.

A spirit that is capable of holding light has a rhythm and vibration that is in phase with the frequencies of light. As a person's spirit loses its ability to hold light it has to go through this reality of sloth and depression as its rhythm and vibration cease to exist; as if its rhythm and vibration becomes a flat line. Then as a person learns to be motivated by pride and envy he or she will learn to create a spirit that is capable of holding the darkness that is a reflection of the hurtful things he or she does or did to others. This is why this dark black part of the kingdom of the heavens is referred to as the abyss.

The following is a quote from the prophecy that describes this fifth church of Sardis:

> *"And to the angel of the church in Sardis write: These things says he that has the seven spirits of God and the seven stars: I know thy works, that thou hast a name that thou livest, and art dead. Become wakeful, and strengthen the things that remain that are about to die. For I have not found thy works fulfilled before my God. Remember therefore how thou hast received and heard, and watch and repent. If therefore thou wilt not be wakeful, I will come as a thief, and thou shalt not know at what hour I will come upon thee. But thou hast a few names in Sardis who have not defiled their garments, and they shall walk with me in white, for they are worthy.*
> *He that overcomes, he shall be clothed in white raiment, and I will not blot his name out of the book of life, and I will confess his name before my Father and before his angels. He that has an ear, let him hear what the Spirit says to the churches."* (Rev. 3.1 – 3.6)

PHILADELPHIA (THE SPIRIT OF PRIDE)

The phrase that describes this church as the church of pride is,

> *"Behold, I will give to them of the synagogue of Satan, that say that they are Jews, and are not, but do lie: behold, I will make them come and worship before thy feet, and they shall know that I have loved thee."* (Rev. 3.9)

In the darkness of this abyss a person lives with a sense of being consumed by a need to be at the center of life. It is more than a need to be at the center of attention. It is this self-centered nature that is the essence of pride.

This state of mind is defined by a need to achieve a sense of who they are. When a person lives with a light based spirit there was no need to know who you are. In a light based reality you accept you for who you are and there is no need to prove yourself. But in a darker reality, until a person fulfills this need prove how good they are, they are motivated to prove they can do something or even anything. It is this need that motivates them in such a way that the need to win is all that matters. This all-consuming reality will rule your life like a king that rules his nation. There is an interesting twist that occurs as a person lives with this king in his or her life. This twist is that we believe that, if we can just accomplish one more objective, climb one step higher, gain more power and control over others that we will become the king. This is how an obsessive or narcissistic personality forms.

Earlier we talked about how we rationalize in our mind that it is ok to do hurtful things to others. This rationalizing grows into an even larger reality in this state of mind. To believe that you can reverse the role of this king that rules your life by actually becoming the king occurs as a person is evolving into one of the darkest levels of this church. Part of this rationalization is to believe that if you can become the ruler you will never have a problem that you cannot deal with or overcome. The challenge to this reality in life is that you are actually becoming weaker in spirit and less capable of dealing with the real problems in your life; the real problems in your life center on your issues and the depth of the loves that were lost throughout your life.

When the prophecy states that God will make others come and worship at your feet and they shall know that I have loved thee is this twist in reality that we are talking about. To think that love is about others paying tribute to you because you rule over them is what the depth of this church of pride is describing.

The following is a quote from the prophecy that describes this sixth church of Philadelphia:

> *"And to the angel of the church in Philadelphia write: These things says he that is holy, he that is true, he that has the key of David, he that opens and no one shall shut, and shuts and no one shall open; I know thy works; behold, I have placed before thee an open door, that no one can shut; because thou hast a little strength, and hast kept my word and hast not denied my name.*
> *Behold, I will give to them of the synagogue of Satan, that say that they are Jews, and are not, but do lie: behold, I will make them come and worship before thy feet, and they shall know that I have loved thee. Because thou hast kept the word of my patience, I also will keep thee from the hour of temptation that shall come on all the world, to try them that dwell on the earth.*

I come quickly: hold fast that which thou hast, that no one take thy crown. He that overcomes, I will make him a pillar in the temple of my God, and he shall go out no more, and I will write upon him the name of my God and the name of the city of my God, the new Jerusalem that comes down out of heaven from my God, and my new name
He that has an ear, let him hear what the Spirit says to the churches." (Rev. 3.7 – 3.13)

LAODICEA (THE SPIRIT OF ENVY)

"The phrase that describes this church as the church of envy is, "I know thy works, that thou art neither cold nor hot. I would that thou wert either cold or hot.
So because thou art lukewarm, and neither cold nor hot, I will vomit thee out of my mouth.
Because thou sayest: I am rich and have abundance and have need of nothing, and knowest not that thou art wretched and pitiable and poor and blind and naked, ..." (Rev. 4.15 – 4.17)

To live with jealousy and envy in your life is to feel little or nothing in your life. It is like your spirit is no longer capable of experiencing any depth of emotion. To have access into the kingdom of the heavens a spirit must first have this fundamental reality in it. At the least a spirit entering this realm of existence must want to have the knowledge of good and evil – this desire to learn will allow it into our world. Then it is up to creation and this individual spirit to work together in such a way as to begin its quest into a lighter existence. Anyone's personal spirit that does not have what it takes to begin its quest into the light will leave this realm and be left to its continued existence "in the deep" of a darker reality. In the deep is in reference to a phrase used on the first day of creation from the book of Genesis. This is what is meant by the statement, "I will vomit you out of my mouth". (Rev. 4.16)

In this last and darkest state of mind is where the healing of a broken spirit begins. Once a spirit and soul start down this path of disintegration it must continue to be broken down until it reaches this darkest pit of the abyss. Only after it has reached this weakest point in its existence can it effectively re-create itself and eventually have the strength it needs to exist with light in it. This happens to each of us individually and all of mankind collectively. Collectively we existed in this darkest reality during the times of Jesus.

Envy and pride work together in your life to create an interesting dynamic. When your spirit is so weak that you can feel hurt by others simply because

1) they have more things or friends or just joy and happiness than you, you will feel weak and powerless
2) others people can create the perception that you have less than they do, you will feel weak and powerless

This feeling of being weak in spirit is very motivating and can cause a person to act in a very hurtful and vengeful way. When a person's spirit is very weak and then to have a person try to make him or her feel weaker is a very bad reality for both people involved. This is how one person tries to rule over another. When one person's pride evolves into such a reality that he or she needs to destroy someone else in order to feel good about him-self or her-self is when the need to be a king has consumed him or her. It is this state of mind, of being consumed by the spirit of envy that is deadly to your spirit and to those around you. To need to take someone else's happiness in order to feel good about your-self is one of the weakest realities of life. The reality of this state of mind is that you do not become the king or ruler over others. Instead of ruling over others, you lose even more of your light as you become jealous of what others have and need to take whatever makes them feel good. Now your unhappiness grows and is dependent on taking what makes others happy.

The following is a quote from the prophecy that describes this seventh church of Laodicea:

"And to the angel of the church in Laodicea write: These things says the Amen, the witness that is faithful and true, the beginning of the creation of God; I know thy works, that thou art neither cold nor hot. I would that thou wert either cold or hot.
So because thou art lukewarm, and neither cold nor hot, I will vomit thee out of my mouth.
Because thou sayest: I am rich and have abundance and have need of nothing, and knowest not that thou art wretched and pitiable and poor and blind and naked,
I counsel thee to buy of me gold purified in fire, that thou mayest be rich, and white raiment, that thou mayest be clothed, and the shame of thy nakedness may not be made manifest, and to anoint thy eyes with eyesalve, that thou mayest see. As many as I love I rebuke and chasten: be zealous therefore, and repent. Behold, I stand at the door and knock: if any one hear my voice and open the door, I will come in to him and will sup with him and he with me.
He that overcomes, I will give to him to sit with me in my throne, as I also overcame and sat down with my Father in his throne.
He that has an ear, let him hear what the Spirit says to the churches." (Rev. 3.14- 3.22)

If the kingdom of the heavens is the bridge or playing field on which spirit creates its-self; then the descriptions of the seven churches that you just read also describe seven parts of the kingdom of the heavens. Since these seven parts represent the darker side of the heavens (candlesticks) then the lighter side of the heavens has seven parts of it that are the polar opposite in light. This is best explained as the journey into darkness and the quest to find the light of the heavens. This is what the prophecy is all about. The best explanation of the quest to find the light of the heavens is through the first thing that Jesus taught – the Beatitudes.

THE BEATITUDES

The Bible tells Jesus' first lesson in a speech referred to as, "The Sermon on the Mount". The first thing he talks about is called, "The Beatitudes". This lesson teaches us the 14 steps that we will naturally grow through as we evolve through the 14 parts of the kingdom of the heavens (7 parts in dark and 7 parts in light).

There are 14 Beatitudes' they are:

The first seven explain the quest out of the darker side of the heavens. This is how we cleanse our spirit of the darkness of our creation.

1) *"Blessed are the poor in spirit; for theirs is the kingdom of the heavens."* (Matthew 5.3)
2) *"Blessed are the meek; for they shall inherit the earth."* (Matthew5.4)
3) *"Blessed are they that mourn; for they shall be comforted."* (Matthew 5.5)
4) *"Blessed are they that hunger and thirst for righteousness; for they shall be filled."* (Matthew 5.6)
5) *"Blessed are the merciful; for they shall receive mercy."* (Matthew 5.7)
6) *"Blessed are the pure in heart; for they shall see God."* (Matthew 5.8)
7) *"Blessed are the peacemakers; for they shall be called sons of God."* (Matthew 5.9)

These last seven explain the quest to create and hold the light that is in our spirit.

8) *"Blessed are they that are persecuted for righteousness' sake; for theirs is the kingdom of the heavens."* (Matthew 5.10)
9) *"Blessed are you when they shall reproach you, and persecute you, and say every evil thing against you falsely for my sake."* (Matthew 5.11)
10) *"Rejoice, and be exceeding glad; for great is your reward in the heavens; for so persecuted they the prophets that were before you."* (Matthew 5.12)
11) *"You are the salt of the earth; but if the salt shall have become tasteless, by what means shall it be salted? It is then good for nothing but, after being cast out, to be trod upon by men."* (Matthew 5.13)
12) *"You are the light of the world. A city that lies upon a mountain cannot be hid:"* (Matthew 5.14)
13) *"neither do men light a lamp and put it under the measure, but on the lampstand, and it gives light to all that are in the house."* (Matthew 5.15)
14) *"So let your light shine before men, that they may see your good works, and glorify your Father who is in the heavens."* (Matthew 5.16)

The following is an explanation of the Beatitudes as they tell the story of a healing heart and spirit on its quest to find light.

1) Blessed are the poor in spirit.

   To be poor in the spirit of envy is to reject its trappings and the feelings of being less than others. To realize that you can feel good without needing others to make you feel good about your self is the first step in becoming poor in the spirit of envy.

2) Blessed are the meek

   To be meek or humble is the state of mind needed to reverse the effects of the spirit of pride.

3) Blessed are they that mourn

   To mourn or to cry is to release the sadness that exists in your spirit so you can begin to create a stronger spirit. When you mourn you are accepting the sadness that lies within your spirit. When you do not allow yourself to mourn you deny the reality of this sadness that lives in your spirit. This will reverse the effects of living with the spirit of sloth.

4) Blessed are they that hunger and thirst for righteousness; for they shall be filled.

   To hunger for righteousness is the depth of commitment that is needed to transform your spirit from dark to light. As you drifted into the darkness of the abyss it was only natural that you were motivated by cravings. These cravings were a very powerful commitment to what you created. Now, when you are ready to transform your spirit back into the light of the heavens you must really want it; you must hunger for righteousness. To hunger for righteousness is the reality that is needed to cleanse your spirit so you can prepare it to hold light. When you hunger for forgiveness you will have that something in your spirit needed to commit to re-creating your spirit. When you hunger for righteousness you will fill your spirit with that which you hunger for. When you hunger for forgiveness you will create forgiveness in your spirit. Forgiveness is what will create the strength your spirit needs to hold light.

5) Blessed are the merciful; for they shall receive mercy.

   Now that we are capable of creating through a light-based spirit it is only natural that the light in our spirit and love in our hearts will make us feel merciful towards others. Since we now have the power to create through our spirit we can now create a merciful spirit. To be merciful is to begin to re-create your live of self. To treat others in a merciful way is to reverse the effects of manipulating and deceiving people. To be merciful is to create mercy in your spirit. It is important to note that you have to hunger for righteousness before you can create a merciful spirit. You have to create with a hunger in your heart in order to re-create your spirit.

6) Blessed are the pure in heart; for they shall see God.

As a merciful spirit continues to create a more positive reality in our lives we will become more pure in heart. Our emotions will be more positive and our intentions more pure. A pure heart will allow you to understand God and how creation works through you. At this point in the evolution of your spirit, you will become more aware (learn to sense and feel) of the feelings of others around you with greater clarity. To reverse the effects of greed is to learn to love others especially family and close friends.

7) Blessed are the peacemakers; for they shall be called sons of God.

As our heart becomes pure we will feel a sense of peace in our lives. This is not about demanding that others live their life the way I do, so I can have my peace. It is about accepting others for who they are regardless of what they say, think or do to me or to others. Peace of mind will always come before peace on earth. With love in your heart, acceptance in your spirit and peace of mind to guide your life's decisions you will begin to grow into a higher consciousness as you become the son of God. It is important to note that a merciful spirit allows you to love others and this is when you sense the truth about God and the collective spirit of mankind. Then as you find peace of mind you become one with the collective spirit of mankind at a higher level than when you lived in a darker reality. Living in a darker reality is to be disconnected from the collective spirit of mankind. The polarity of a darker spirit repels your body, spirit and soul as well as the spirit of others. To be in a polarizing relationship is to be in a relationship with someone who has a weaker spirit. Polarizing relationships create a weaker relations ship and collective spirits.

The first seven Beatitudes are the seven steps needed to cleanse your spirit of the darkness of its existence. These are the things that we will do as our spirit begins to change from a darker polarity. When the prophecy refers to the phrase repent and overcome it is referring to these beatitudes. The first seven beatitudes are about repenting (forgiving) and the last seven are about overcoming (living with love).

The following seven steps are what we will do as we overcome the lifestyle that was the reality we lived with when our spirit was weaker. As we change the way we live we will re-create our spirit in such a way as to hold light and then to live with it as we share it with others.

8) Blessed are they that are persecuted for righteousness' sake; for theirs is the kingdom of the heavens.

This step in the process is linked to the fourth beatitude. The fourth beatitude is about hungering for righteousness so you can cleanse your spirit. This eighth beatitude is about creating and living with a righteous spirit. When others want to degrade you or talk about you behind your back because you are doing the right thing with your life; you are being persecuted. Stand strong and believe in you; live for what you believe in and just do what you know is the right thing to do in life. Do this and your spirit will evolve into this greater light of the heavens.

9) Blessed are you when they shall reproach you, and persecute you, and say every evil thing against you falsely for my sake.

As you live to make the world a better place those that do not want to change or see these changes come into the world will become more aggressive in their efforts to prevent you from evolving. As you evolve your spirit will naturally have a higher vibration. This higher vibration will make others around you feel uncomfortable and they will strive to prevent you from continuing on your quest to find your light. When a person's spirit is filled with lust they talk about other people; they talk behind someone's back and try to get them to change who they are by making them feel as if they are doing something wrong. When a person tries to leave the church of lust those that are still in that state of mind will only do the best they can with what they have; so they will say every evil thing they can against you.

10) Rejoice, and be exceeding glad; for great is your reward in the heavens; for so persecuted they the prophets that were before you.

As your spirit and soul evolve into the higher states of mind that live in the light side of the kingdom of the heavens you will naturally grow into a happier state of mind. It is like you get to a point when you realize that your happiness is a new reality in your life. It is like you can just be happy and not need anything or anyone to make you happy; your happiness is just there and it stays with you all the time. This is the way a child experiences life before the realities of life guide him into a reality that needs things and people to make him happy. You get these better feelings because your spirit now feeds off the blood of life that comes from the kingdom of the heavens. As your spirit heals the seven parts of your spirit become cups that hold the light of the kingdom of the heavens. As your cups (spirit) fill with light and you feel the love that is this light; it is like drinking the blood of life. At this point you have achieved peace of mind and should celebrate it.

11) You are the salt of the earth; but if the salt shall have become tasteless, by what means shall it be salted? It is then good for nothing but, after being cast out, to be trod upon by men.

As unconditional love grows in your spirit you become the salt of the earth. As your spirit evolves into this greater light it (you) will have a very positive impact on the collective spirit of mankind. In this way you are the salt that improves the collective spirit of mankind. Your light is now capable of shining brightly as you learn to live with your light and love and then to share it with others.
Also when the collective spirit of mankind has evolved to a point where a significant number of people all exist with a spirit filled with peace the earth will be filled with salt. The earth is a reflection of how far the collective spirit has evolved into the heavens. In the beginning it was void and had no form. As we evolve in to this higher light of the heavens the earth becomes filled with the spirit of who **we are.**
At this point you have to use it or you will lose it. It is about finding others that you can befriend and live with so you can continue to feed off the light of the kingdom of the heavens and then share it with others.

12) You are the light of the world. A city that lies upon a mountain cannot be hid:

As a person learns to accept the light in his spirit to become a part of his life he will naturally share that light with others. As you share your love and light with others you become a beacon of light within the collective spirit and other people in the world. In this way you are the light of the world.

13) Neither do men light a lamp and put it under the measure, but on the lampstand, and it gives light to all that are in the house.

As you learn to live with purpose in your life, your spirit will become filled with the light of your purpose. This is when the candlesticks that described the darker reality of the churches changes into a lampstand. The positive nature of your purpose is the lampstand and the passion (love and light) you put into this purpose is the light that glows within the house you are creating. It is like you are creating a home that will house the spirit of the purpose of your creation.

14) So let your light shine before men, that they may see your good works, and glorify your Father who is in the heavens.

As your life becomes filled with purpose it is only natural that your spirit will become stronger as your purpose fills your life. Now, your purpose will shine brightly and your personal spirit will be brighter.

Now the healing of your spirit and soul is complete and you function as one in body, spirit and soul. As you learn to live with a whole and complete body, spirit and soul you will learn to say what you think and do what comes naturally to you. Sincerity is one of the most gratifying realities that come with living with a light based spirit. You will not have to think before you speak or act. To just react to what you feel of see and to know that your actions are constructive in nature is synchronicity. When your body, spirit and soul act as one being in love and light you have created your grail cup; your Holy Grail. This synchronicity will guide you as you live with a greater purpose in your life.

There are several levels of synchronicity.

The first level we learn to live with is when our body, spirit and soul work together.

The next level is when we learn to work with others and are in sync with the thoughts, words and actions of others.

An even higher level of synchronicity is when we are guided by a purpose that feeds us feelings that guide our thoughts, words and actions. At this level we learn to accomplish goals and objectives with a sense of ease and rhythm in our lives.

The highest level of synchronicity is when we work together in small or large groups as one in body, spirit and soul. This synchronicity occurs when we all live in the brightest light of the heavens. This brightest light of the heavens will only exist when we create it because we are all collectively guided by a sense of purpose that will create the light of our thoughts, words and actions.

CHAPTER 3

THE LAMB AND THE BOOK WITH SEVEN SEALS

Then there was man (Adam and Eve are now clothed in skin)

1. the lamb (the evolution of mankind)
2. the book with 7 seals (the book of the knowledge of dark and light)
3. the seven seals
4. the 12 tribes of 12,000 members per tribe that are the 144,000 that are sealed by the 7 seals
5. the 7 angels with 7 trumpets
6. the mystery of the angel with the little book that tastes sweet in ST. John's mouth but turns bitter in his stomach

CREATING THE SPIRIT OF HUMAN NATURE IS ONE OF THE FIRST CREATIONS OF CREATION.

WHEN THE SEALS THAT SEALED OUR FATE WERE RELEASED FROM THE BOOK OF KNOWLEDGE OF LOVE AND LIGHT THE SPIRIT OF HUMAN NATURE WAS DESCRIBED AS FOUR RIDERS ON HORSES.

IN THIS SECOND SCENE OF THE PROPHECY THE COLLECTIVE SPIRIT AND SOUL OF MANKIND HAVE EXISTED IN DARKNESS. MANKND IS SEARCHING FOR A WAY TO CREATE A BETTER EXISTENCE BUT CANNOT FIND THEIR WAY INTO THE LIGHT OF THE HEAVENS. THEY TRY TO OPEN THE BOOK OF KNOWLEDGE OF LOVE AND LIGHT BUT ARE NOT ABLE TO RELEASE THE SEALS THAT SEAL THEIR FATE.

THE PROPHECY REFERS TO A LAMB THAT IS ABLE TO RELEASE THESE SEVEN SEALS THAT SEAL A BOOK. THE LAMB IS THE MISSING LINK IN A SPIRITUAL SENSE. WHEN MOSES DEMONSTRATED UNCONDITIONAL LOVE BY LEADING THE ISRAELITES INTO THE DESERT HE RELEASED THE SEALS AND THE POWER OF CREATION WAS RELEASED INTO MANKINDS EXISTENCE. MOSES LEADING THE ISRAELITES INTO THE DESERT WAS PART OF A PLAN TO HELP THE FAMILY OF ISRAEL TO LEARN TO CREATE LOVE NAD LIHGT IN FUTURE GENERATIONS.

THE PLAN WAS THAT THE OLDER GENERATIONS OF ISRAELITES THAT WERE FILLED WITH HATRED AND RAGE WOULD DIE IN THE DESERT. THEY WERE FILLED WITH ANGER, HATRED AND RAGE BECAUSE OF THE WAY THEY WERE TREATED BY THE EGYPTIANS.

THEN MOSES WOULD TEACH THE YOUNGER GENERATIONS HOW TO RE-CREATE THEIR SPIRITS AND THEN LEARN TO LIVE IN THE LIGHT AGAIN.

BUT MOSES DID NOT HAVE THE OPPORTUNITY TO TEACH THEM.

SINCE THE PLAN DID NOT GO ACCORDING TO PLAN JESUS CAME TO FIX THE PROBLEM. WHEN JESUS LIVED HIS LIFE TO FORGIVE AND LOVE HE CREATED THE PATH INTO THE LIGHT THAT DID NOT EXIST. AS HE LIVED WITH A PASSION TO FORGIVE AND LOVE HE CREATED A FORGIVING SPIRIT. THIS FORGIVING SPIRIT WAS THE SEED THAT WAS PLANTED IN THE COLLECTIVE SPIRIT OF MANKIND AND IN THE AMBIENT SPIRIT THAT WAS CREATED BY MANKIND.

NOW 2,000 YEARS LATER THIS SEED HAS GROWN IN OUR HEARTS AND WE ARE LEARNING TO FORGIVE AND TO LOVE AGAIN.

FOR THOUSANDS OF YEARS MANKIND HAS BEEN EVOLVING INTO A LIGHTER REALITY. AS WE HAVE EVOLVED WE HAVE BECOME CONSCIOUSLY AWARE OF RULES AND LAWS OF NATURE. AS WE CONTINUE TO EVOLVE WE WILL GAIN A GREATER UNDERSTANDING OF THESE LAW OF CREATION, PROCESSES AND REALITIES OF CREATION.

In this second scene there is a lot going on. Mankind becomes a part of the evolution of the spirit and soul's existence. The body, spirit and soul are learning to live and exist in a broken reality. The darkness that was only over the deep is now a part of the kingdom of the heavens; fear, anger, hatred and rage are the primary emotions through which mankind created. The rage, ire, distain and wrath of the abyss created the first ambient spirit of mankind – the spirit of Babylon. Over time the "spirit of Babylon" grew into a greedy, gluttonous, lust filled spirit that consumed the world and the lives of everyone that lived so many thousands of years ago. While filled with this spirit of Babylon people accepted a reality that things like genocide and murder were acceptable behaviors. This darkest spirit of mankind's creations entered the spirit of the Israelites after they left their Holy Land and went to live in Egypt. The Egyptian Pharaoh invited them to move to Egypt and then passed away. His son was the next in line to rule the Middle East. His son implemented a plan to destroy the spirits of the Israelites. This was the beginning of the darkest existence of the Israelites.

This spirit of Babylon will continue until we change it. It will continue until <u>we change</u>.

THE LAMB (THE EVOLUTION OF MANKIND)

You should now start to realize that the images and symbols of the prophecy each have several meanings. Each image and symbol can teach us something about the body, spirit and soul as well as how we work individually and collectively through the kingdom of the heavens. Each of these scenes describes a time when the spirit of man was dark, learning to live in the light or maintain their light. For example the lamb represented the evolution of mankind as well as the evolution of the spirit and soul as Moses and Jesus helped the Israelites. As any nation learns the lessons that come from its spiritual leaders and that nation creates a positive spirit they will impact the collective spirit of mankind and the world. This is the lesson of the lamb. We are the lamb because we experience life and impact the collective spirit of mankind. Moses, Jesus, Mohammad, Buddha and other prophets are remembered throughout history for their impact on the teachings of spirituality. Moses and Jesus did something very special though; at a time when love did not exist in the spirit of man they brought unconditional love into the collective spirit of man.

In the end we all have to follow the one law of creation and that is, "Love completely and the share that love with your neighbors". This is what Jesus meant when he was asked, "*What is the greatest commandment?*" he replied, "*you must love God with all your heart, all your mind, all your soul and strength; and you must love your neighbor as yourself*". He was telling them to love completely and then to share that love with others. He was telling us to love God, love ourselves and then to love others. The process of re-creation will create a love of God in your spirit; then when you love yourself you will be able to create a better life for you and impact the collective spirit of mankind in a positive way; finally, when you share your love with others you co-create a better world for everyone because the spirit you co-create will create a more positive ambient spirit in the world.

In the prophecy the lamb releases the seven seals and then seven images appear to St. John. These seven images (including what are commonly referred to as the four horsemen) represent the spirit of mankind at that moment when mankind was sealed into a darker reality. It represents the spirits of the seven parts of the kingdom of the heavens that ruled over mankind's existence until these seven seals were released. These seven seals describe human nature as it existed during Moses life. They are also the seals that sealed the fate of the Israelites. Only after all of mankind lived in a collective spirit that was in this depth of darkness were we able to begin to re-create ourselves.

THE BOOK WITH 7 SEALS (THE BOOK OF THE KNOWLEDGE OF DARK AND LIGHT)

The book represents the knowledge of both light and dark because when a person's spirit is creating the seals as he loses his light he is learning to live without light; while releasing the seals and evolving from dark to light he is learning to live with light in his spirit and love in his heart again. This is why the prophecy says there is writing on both sides of its pages.

This book does not present us with knowledge in the same sense as we might expect. It is not like going to school and learning history, biology, math or science. It is more like a state of knowing or being aware of who you are and the spirit of others around you as well it is the consciousness you gain access to when you learn to apply yourself to a purpose. To live with a purpose to do something that and then to just know what you need to know when you need to know it is another way of being consciously aware. This is how the gift of knowledge (the gift of knowing) works. It is about learning how to live with your spirit and soul as you grow into the light of the love you will feel as your spiritual quest takes you into a lighter state of mind.

People live in a darker state of mind with a spirit and soul that is separated from their consciousness. This is when people refer to their conscience as being a part of their subconscious mind. This will change as we release these seals and learn to live with consciousness. As they live without the depth of love they are capable of living with they deny their feelings and the consciousness that accompanies it. As your spirit and soul evolve into a lighter state they work together through you in a different way. When in a darker state of mind people might rely on deception and manipulation to get what they want, need, desire or crave. When living with a lighter spirit living with sincerity and purpose becomes a priority and then a way of life. This is a very evolutionary reality in our lives. It is not something that we have to make happen; these changes will evolve. The important thing to remember is as you evolve into a greater emotional reality you will learn to just let things happen in your life. It is natural to resist these changes and to resist the positive emotions that come with this stage of evolution.

This book of knowledge of love and light teaches several realities:

1) Feelings that come to your through your spirit and how the emotions you emit create the spirit of who you are at any moment in time
2) A state of knowing that comes from your soul
3) A state of awareness that comes from being one in spirit and soul allowing you to discern the spirit that is in the air around you.
4) The ability to manage your feelings and the state of mind you create in order access information pertaining to whatever you want to know.

When a darker reality exists in a person's life his body, spirit and soul do not function as one. The body has to function in a world with laws and rules that guide our behaviors while its spirit is weak and exists in a collective spirit that is not strong enough to present itself in society. It is like when in a dark state of mind we hide our spirit as we wear a mask of indifference that is supposed to prevent people from knowing the darkness of our thoughts and feelings. This state of denial is why people live in denial of their spirit while trying to hide their true feelings so others will accept them in society. The mind is thought of as something that is beneath the surface of their reality; this is the subconscious mind.

In this darker state of mind people strive to have what they need to survive. This conscious reality is the "I Need" consciousness. As a person grows beyond the "I Need" consciousness he or she will grow into the "I Am" consciousness. Beyond the "I Am" conscious are the "We Are" consciousness and "We Are Us" consciousness. The final level of pure consciousness is the "We Are God" consciousness.

The "I Am" consciousness is a state of mind in which people begin to realize their power as creators; it is a state of mind where we grow from being smart to trusting our senses and developing a sense of trust in our thoughts and feelings. It is a state of spirit and soul where we can just know a truth without the need to think or over think an issue. This realization that we can just know is a reality shift that will allow us to grow into a better state of mind and create a better world for all. To just simply know the answer to a problem and to have faith that the truth will appear when it should appear is a skill that people will develop while the collective consciousness experiences its existence in this lesser and greater light of the heavens. To have faith is a higher level of this consciousness. The "I AM" consciousness is about finding your-self and knowing how good you really are and can be. One of the most important things to remember about this reality of consciousness is that you are <u>learning</u> to just be you, instead of trying to be the person you think others want you to be. As you accept you for who you are you acquire the awareness that you create the spirit of who you are at any moment in time. The power of creation comes from knowing who you are and then just being you and setting your-self free to just be you. This is the power of "I AM", it is the power that comes with just being you.

As people learn to have faith in creation and how it works and then learn to have faith in those around us we are entering the "We Are" consciousness. To accept that you will know what you need to know when you need to know it is a big part of developing the skill to just know a truth. When we are dealing with a situation and feel a need to know something right now but the answer does not come to us is a test in faith. To have faith in that what I need will be here when I need it is a big part of the process of evolving through the greater light of the heavens. As a person lives with a spirit capable of holding a bright light the challenges of learning to have faith in all its forms will become a part of your life.

As a person learns to forgive himself and others as well, will seek forgiveness from those he hurt, then the potential to gain clarity in his or her senses will evolve.

We have been talking about the ability to discern spirit and know things about others throughout this book. The following is a list of that which you will sense, feel and know as your spirit becomes more pure and you gain the clarity needed to sense and feel spirit:

A state of knowing that is love-based consciousness
An awareness of what others think and feel
An awareness of your personal spirit (thoughts and feelings)
An awareness of the spirit of others
An awareness of the thoughts and feelings of the collective spirit
An awareness of the ambient spirits that exist in the air around you throughout your day to day life

In order to fully discuss the concept of awareness we must consider three aspects of awareness:

Being unconsciously aware of your spirit and soul
Being aware of your subconscious mind
Being consciously aware of your spirit and soul as well as the spirit of others around you, collective spirit of mankind and the ambient spirit of our creations

AS THE COLLECTIVE SPIRIT OF MANKIND EVOLVES WE WILL LEARN GREATER TRUTHS

HOW GREATER TRUTHS ARE ENTERING OUR CONSCIOUSENSS TODAY

As we have been evolving for the past several hundred years we have been learning about spirituality. We have learned about concepts like the continuity of life, incarnation and reincarnation and many laws of nature and universal laws. It is only natural that creation and evolution would introduce these thoughts into our consciousness. It is only natural that these concepts will transform into a greater understanding of them over time. For example:

1) Continuity of life – nature and the universe is about each and every one of us having a life and a spiritual existence. When a person's life ends it does not mean that their spirits existence ends. The continuity of life states that the spirit of all people will reincarnate into this world again so we can continue our spirits journey. Life is about our spirit and souls human experience.

   In creation the concept of continuity of life is more about the collective spirit of mankind and how it evolves through the kingdom of the heavens. Lifetime after lifetime and generation after generation we transform the collective spirit of mankind as it grows through the kingdom of the heavens.

2) Incarnation and Reincarnation – In nature and the universe reincarnation is about an individual person's spirit returning to another life as it continues its journey in nature. In creation this is true but with a little twist. In creation a person's spirit is broken into many pieces while we struggle to survive in a darker collective reality. This means that we enter the world as one spirit and then die leaving behind several. Therefore we are no longer the same spirit we were when we started and these new spirits will incarnate (or reincarnate) into future lives as different people. Then as the collective spirit of mankind evolves into a greater light these parts of a broken spirit will naturally reincarnate as we begin our quest to become one again. Knowing how this reality of incarnation works sheds a new light on the concept of the continuity of life and reincarnation.

3) The Law of Choice – Many people believe we all have a choice in our lives to make our lives better. They say that it is just a matter of choosing to be different and you will be able to change. As if it is that easy. It is that easy for people with spirits that have already evolved through one of the levels of creation and live in a higher reality.

   In creation if a person has created a forgiving spirit he or she will not have to try to forgive others or even think about it; forgiveness will just happen. A person with an accepting spirit will not judge others or even have an expectation of others; you will just accept him or her. When a person's is in a gray area still developing light in their spirit and learning to not judge others he or she will have to choose to not judge others. This is where the reality of creation differs from the law of nature. The law says we can choose. The reality of creation says that while learning we will have to make choices that will define the spirit we are creating. These choices are no longer a reality in our lives when we have successfully recreated our spirit. In creation a person that lives in a darker reality does not have the capability to choose to just be different. A person living with depression or anxieties cannot just choose to not be depressed and or have anxieties. It is not to say that this is not a good idea to do or that you have to just accept depression or anxieties in your life. The reality in creation is that there is a lot more to it than just choosing to make a change in your life. A person in a darker reality has to choose to do a lot of soul searching and a lot of work to transform their spirit as well he or she must have their prodigal son moment and then begin the processes of re-creating their spirit. Without this moment in creation when you accept that there is something in your life that created this reality in your spirit you will not be able to transform your spirit. Without this transformative moment in your life you will not have the inner strength needed to overcome the depressive or anxious nature of your spirit. This is not to say that you have to just accept depression or anxieties in your life.

This subtle but important reality in creation is more about recognizing that people who have developed a healthier spirit can choose to fill their spirit with light and love or anger and darkness. It is a moment by moment reality that only those that have a light spirit will be able to live with.

In creation the reality of change has to come before choice can become a reality in your life and the need to choose goes away after you have re-created your spirit.

As we have been evolving into a lighter spirit the awareness of our personal and the collective spirit has naturally entered our consciousness. The first awareness brought with it information we could accept based on the amount of light that existed in the collective spirit. As individuals we live within the collective spirit. The collective spirit contains a range of emotional content. Within this range are people with an emotional content that is at the higher end of the collective. When a person's personal spirit evolves to this higher level he or she will have access this knowledge or conscious awareness. After some people grew to this higher level of spirit and consciousness they grew to understand things like the laws of nature and the universe.

Now, several generations later we have a greater light in our spirit and the capability to have a higher consciousness. This book explains the realities of creation and evolution with a deeper understanding of the spirit and soul and the reality of how change occurs in our spirits thereby bringing a greater awareness into our consciousness.

Future generations will bring an even greater light into what the current generations know and a greater understanding of nature, the universe, creation and evolution. Whether we are talking about spiritual realities and the knowledge that enters our consciousness related to it or we are talking about physics, science or psychology as a greater light enters our spirit a greater consciousness enters our thoughts. This is how we make this world a better place generation after generation and lifetime after lifetime, through creation and evolution.

This book with seven seals also represents the plan to use creation and evolution to allow the body, spirit and soul to grow through the kingdom of the heavens and into the kingdom of God. It is a plan to transform this darkness that was the deep into an angel. The plan is simple through the love and light of the body, spirit and soul the collective spirit will re-create its self and evolve. The plan includes a periodic follow-up to make sure the plan is going according to plan. The first time the angels checked to see how the plan was going was just before Jesus was born.

THE SEVEN SEALS

In the first scene the collective soul of mankind was seen as walking among seven candlesticks. This was the consciousness of mankind's collective soul when the spirit and soul were broken. Throughout many lifetimes and generations mankind continued to create its existence through this darker reality as the soul existed in the darkness of the kingdom of the heavens. The first scene also showed the collective spirit of mankind's existence in the darkness of the seven churches. In this second scene the collective soul is represented as the book and that which we created while living in the darkness of the seven churches are these seven seals. These seven seals represent both the collective spirit of mankind and the seven parts of the kingdom of the heavens that existed at the moment when Moses demonstrated unconditional love for the Israelites as he led them through the desert.

The seven seals represent human nature and the realities of how mankind lived when the seals were released.

This scene also has seven trumpets in it. These seven trumpets represent the collective spirit of mankind throughout many lifetimes after Moses died. They represent the reality that existed in the collective spirit of people for a time period of about 1,700 years. After about 1,700 years the powers that be in creation realized the plan was not going according to plan. Jesus was born to determine if the plan could work and fix what was wrong or seal mankind into a darker reality again. You will learn more about how Jesus fixed the problem when you read about the 6th angel with the 6th trumpet.

THE SEVEN SEALS THAT SEAL THE BOOK OF KNOWLEDGE OF LOVE AND LIGHT

The first image of the first scene was the Son of Man walking among seven candlesticks. They represented the soul of man and our consciousness when we lived in the darker reality of the seven unlit candlesticks. This is the darker collective consciousness that impacts the consciousness we receive through our soul's consciousness. The seven candlesticks represent the seven parts of the kingdom of the heavens which is the source of all feelings and emotions, thoughts and consciousness. This first scene also included seven churches that represented the seven parts of the collective spirit of mankind that are the seven deadly sins. This first image of the second scene represents the transformation through creation of the images and symbols of the first scene into a new reality that existed at the time of Moses. The book with seven seals represents mankind's consciousness sealed into a darker reality.

These seven seals represent the evolution of the seven churches as mankind's collective spirit created the human nature that is the kingdom of the heavens. The Israelites and mankind created this darker reality of the kingdom of the heavens through our thoughts, words and actions. Through the essence of the seven deadly sins, we created the spirit of the four horsemen and the last three seals. This is how creation works. We create the spirit of who we are and it becomes the kingdom of the heavens; this creates a sense of permanence in the reality that is life for future generations. As you will learn later in this book the prophecy explains how future generations of children enter the world with a brighter spirit and higher consciousness and purpose to make the world a better place. This is why it is so important for future generations to be empowered to create the world in their image.

There is a reality that is an interesting twist that must be understood when interpreting this prophecy. This twist is about the relationship between the angels in the seven churches and these seven seals. If you try to understand the prophecy by reading the first church and then the first seal you will be confused as to how the prophecy links them all together. The four churches are read in sequence as a person loses his or her light. The journey into darkness is about creating a spiritual foundation in fear and anger (wrath) and then greed, lust, gluttony sloth, pride and envy in that order. The loss of compassion (first church) leads to a loss of love of others especially family and close friends (second church) and then love of self (third church) and finally losing love of God, nature and creation (fourth church).

Now here is the twist. When a person is on his or her quest to find their light, the seals will be released in the following order the fourth seal, third seal, second seal and then finally the first seal.

As you read about these seals you will find that the fourth seal is about creating hell on earth; because when a person's spirit exists with the anger of wrath it is the first step into creating in the abyss.

> As we learn to live with fear and anger we lose our love of others especially family and close friends; then we create through buying and selling things with an intention to get the most and give the least with every transaction. This creates the spirit of greed within our personal spirit.
> Then as a person lives with this lack of love of family and close friends it is only a matter of time until we lose our sense of peacefulness within our lives and strive to take peace from others as we learn to use people to get what we want. Using people is the foundation of lust.
> Finally the fourth seal to be released is about creating a conquering spirit that strives to defeat others in every aspect of our lives. Today we think of this darker reality as the

competitive nature of mankind; it is also one of the components of human nature that created hell on earth.

The first four of the seven angels sounding trumpets and holding cups are interpreted in the same order as these four seals. As you can see you have to link these four seals in the reverse order when compared to the first four churches.

The fifth, sixth and seventh seals are all correlated perfectly between the seven churches and seven seals.

THE FOUR HORSEMEN ARE THE FIRST FOUR SEALS

An interesting reality about many interpretations of the prophecy is that there is no reference to four horsemen anywhere in the prophecy. There are four seals that seal a book and each of them has a phrase about a rider on a horse that many have referred to as the four horsemen. You will learn more about these four riders on horses as read the following.

THE FIRST SEAL EVOLVED FROM THE FOURTH CHURCH

"And I saw when the Lamb had opened one of the seven seals, and I heard one of the four living creatures saying as with a voice of thunder: Come. And I saw, and behold, a white horse, and he that sat upon him had a bow, and to him was given a crown, and he went forth conquering and to conquer." (Rev. 6.1 – 6.2)

This first seal releases the suppressive spirit that creates a desire within mankind that makes us feel as if we should conquer one another. This is how we live with a competitive instinct throughout our lives and create hell on earth. It is only by creating a conquering spirit that a person can create through the spirit of this first horseman.

As we live to compete with everything we do in life, we become consumed by the spirits of these horsemen.

THE SECOND SEAL EVOLVED FROM THE THIRD CHURCH

"And when he had opened the second seal. I heard the second living creature saying: Come. And there went forth another horse that was red; and to him that sat on him was given to take peace from the earth, and that they should slay one another: and there was given to him a great sword." (Rev. 6.3 – 6.4)

This second seal releases the destructive spirit that creates a desire within mankind to take peace of mind and any peaceful existence from one another. Only after a person loses his or her own peace of mind can we strive to take peace from others.

THE THIRD SEAL EVOLVED FROM THE SECOND CHURCH

"And when he had opened the third seal, I heard the third living creature saying: Come. And I saw, and behold, a black horse, and he that sat on him had a balance in his hand. And I heard a voice in the midst of the four living creatures, saying: A choenix of wheat for a denarius, and three choenices of barley for a denarius: and see that thou hurt not the oil and the wine." (Rev. 6.5 – 6.6)

This third seal releases the conflict driven reality that manifests in people living to dominate one another right down to every purchase we make when we buy and sell goods and services. When we strive to get the most and give the least with every purchase we make throughout the day we create the spirit of greed in ourselves and in the collective spirit of mankind.

QUESTION

If everything we do creates through the passion, feelings and emotions of every thought, word or action we take; then what are we going to create within our self and in the collective spirit of mankind when we live with a take and give mentality when purchase things?

What are we going to create if we replace this take and give mentality with the spirit of being generous and grateful with everything we say, think and do?

ANSWER:

The spirit of a better world will be created from begin grateful for what we have and generous in giving for what we buy. A better individual spirit will create a better collective spirit; a better collective spirit will create a better ambient spirit.

THE FOURTH SEAL EVOLVED FROM THE FIRST CHURCH

"And when he had opened the fourth seal, I heard the fourth living creature saying: Come. And I saw, and behold, a pale horse, and he that sat on him, his name was death, and hades followed with him; and there was given to them authority over the fourth part of the earth, to kill with the sword and with famine and with death and by the wild beasts of the earth." (Rev. 6.7 – 6.8)

This fourth seal is a reality that exists in spirit. As we live our lives consumed by these four spirits we create our physical reality; this reality is hell on earth. Where the spirit goes the soul follows; therefore when the spirit dies the soul and its consciousness follows and we create hell on earth.

The first four seals relate to the collective spirit of mankind as it is consumed by darkness. It is how our individual spirit is impacted by the collective spirit of mankind.

The moral of the story of these four riders on horses is that you can ride these horses wildly into the darkness of your reality or tame them from within and walk them peacefully into a new reality. Taming them is all about dealing with your issues in life and then creating a light based reality as you live with peace in your life.

The fifth and sixth seals relate to how the collective consciousness worked while the collective spirit is consumed by these first four horsemen. They are about how mankind created when the collective spirit of mankind was filled with the darkness of the four horsemen.

Earlier in this book you read about the Beatitudes. These Beatitudes explain how we will release these seals so we can learn from this book of knowledge of love and light. Four of these seven seals relate to riders on horses that are sent out into mankind to conquer and take peace from mankind. Two of these Beatitudes relate to being merciful and being peacekeepers. The lesson we learn about these horsemen is to tame them by dealing with our issues life; when we hunger for righteousness and are merciful towards others we grow to be pure in heart as we others and become peacekeepers and tame then these wild horses will become tame.

THE FIFTH SEAL

> *"And when he had opened the fifth seal, I saw under the altar the souls of those that had been slain because of the word of God and because of the testimony that they held. And they cried with a loud voice, saying: How long, O Sovereign holy and true, dost thou not judge and avenge our blood on them that dwell on the earth? And there was given to them a white robe, and it was said to them that they should rest yet a while, till the number of their fellow servants and their brethren that should be killed as they had been should be fulfilled."* (Rev. 6.9 – 6.11)

This seal simply meant that the spirit of judgment and vengeance was in the air. This is the reality that resulted from the release of these seals. This was the nature of humanity back in the days when Moses and the Israelites walked in the desert for 40 years. They were rejected by everyone in the Middle East. When they felt rejected by others it created the feeling of being unaccepted. The spirit of judging others is the polar opposite of being filled with the spirit of acceptance.

"Those that had been slain because of the word of God", are those that were hurt and suffered do to the destructive competitive nature of mankind. Remember the statements of this fifth seal represent people as they lived thousands of years ago. This statement also is describing a reality of creation. The reality of creation is that our prayers are answered. When we pray for something, the spirit of that prayer is created. Our thoughts and words that go into the prayer create the spirit of the prayer. As people lived in this destructive reality and were hurt by others they sought vengeance on those that hurt them. This created a reality in creation that perpetuated the destructive nature of mankind. As the Israelites lived a life that destroyed their spirits it was only natural that they would say and do things that were vengeful in nature. This perpetuated the destructive spirit of the reality that was their lives.

For many generations the Israelites tried to maintain a peaceful reality in their lives. When other lords were at war with one another they tried to avoid the conflict that surrounded them. Then when the Egyptians destroyed their spirit they became just like everyone else. When they walked through the desert and were shunned by all the nations of the Middle East their spirits became weaker. This made them more committed to doing whatever it took to survive while living with a spirit that was no longer capable of holding light. They rejected Moses as their leader and then acted on the spirit of survival they created.

This seal is describing the vengeful destructive nature of the spirit of prayers that existed at that moment in time. It existed in the spirit of mankind not just the Israelites.

Today this reality of creation that shapes the future of our lives might be mixed with some vengeance and some with desires to stop the pain that we have been creating for too long and with some prayers that are designed to make this world a better place.

When creating the spirit of a prayer we are creating the spirit of our thoughts and words. When we say a prayer and create the spirit of it, the deeper we reach into the pit of our stomach and really mean what we say, the stronger the spirit of the prayer we create. We have to pray for peace with the same emotional commitment as they did when they sought revenge on those that hurt them.

Today the prophets that live with more evolved spirits are praying for all of mankind to be judged in the same way they were judged. Today those that experience hardships and evolve into a higher light would pray that others will experience life in the same way as they did and be judged in the same way. Then others can join them in a life with a reality that is better than living life consumed by the spirit of the four horsemen. In order to exist with a spirit that is more evolved is to experience the healing process of forgive and live with love (repent and overcome). These prayers are asking that more people experience life in such a way as to realize that they too have to deal with their issues in life and create a spirit filled with light and love.

THE SIXTH SEAL

> *"And I saw when he had opened the sixth seal, and there was a great earthquake, and the sun became black as sackcloth of hair, and the whole of the moon became as blood, and the stars of heaven fell to the earth, as a fig tree casting her untimely figs when shaken by a mighty wind, and the heaven departed as a scroll rolled together, and every mountain and island were moved out of their places. And the kings of the earth and the great men and the officers and the rich and the mighty and every servant and free man hid themselves in the caves and in the rocks of the mountains, and said to the mountains and rocks: Fall upon us and conceal us from the face of him that sits on the throne and from the wrath of the Lamb. For the great day of his wrath has come, and who is able to stand?"* (Rev. 6.12 – 6.17)

This sixth seal describes the way people lived when their spirits were not capable of holding light. It describes a reality where people feel as if they are hiding from the light of the sun. To live as if hiding in a cave waiting for the mountain to fall on you is to hide from the light and to live with so much suffering that you would rather die than to live.

The prayers of the saints of the firth seal create this reality so people with unhealthy spirits can get to the point where they will be able to experience their prodigal son moment.

The problem with this process of healing is that most people could not experience the process of forgive and live with love. When Moses was not able to complete his part of the original plan the light of the heavens closed and people were sealed into this darker reality. When the Israelites left Moses to die in the desert they sealed their fate with this final seal. Moses was their chance to find their way out of the darkness of living with spirits that were sealed in to a darker reality. When they left him in the desert and sought vengeance on those that did not help them when they were in need they created a reality that would stay with them for thousands of years. Leaving Moses in the desert was when they lost their love of family. Moses was a son of Israel and to lose his love was the last straw. When they felt the spirit of that decision their collective spirit made them feel like they should hide from God; hide form themselves.

At this point you need to understand the Law of Creation and the first reality of creation.

The law of creation is to love completely and then share that love with others; Jesus said this when he said,

> "Thou shalt love the Lord thy God with thy whole heart, and with thy whole soul, and with thy whole mind". This is the great and first commandment. A second is like it: Thou shalt love thy neighbor as thyself. On these two commandments hang the whole law and the prophets." (Matthew 22:37 – 40)

The first reality of creation is, "in order to create light you must first live in light". This reality is something that Jesus realized when he came in to the world. Since Moses lost his love for the Israelites and replaced it with anger the seed of love and light that he was planting in the collective spirit of the Israelites was extinguished. Without any light in the collective spirit of mankind others were not able to create their own light. This is why the processes of creation were only going to perpetuate the darkness that existed in the family of Israel. Their personal and collective spirit's inability to hold light stayed that way until Jesus came and planted the two seeds of forgiveness and love in the collective spirit of the Israelites and mankind. This will be discussed later in this book.

This sixth seal describes the lives lived by many people, not just the Israelites, as they lived for about 1,700 years. After about 1,700 years Jesus came and lived with forgiveness and love and even taught people how to create a forgiving spirit and how to live with love. This created in the collective spirit of mankind that which was needed so future generations of people could evolve into a better light.

THE 12 TRIBES OF 12,000 MEMBERS PER TRIBE THAT ARE THE 144,000 THAT ARE SEALED BY THESE SEALS

Six of the seven seals that seal the book of knowledge of love and light are released and then four angels on the four corners of the earth hold the four winds of the earth so they will not blow on the earth until the time is right for them to be released. These four winds are going to take the issues and anger, hatred and rage from the Israelites so the earth can hold them until the Israelites are ready to deal with them in future lifetimes. The Bibles Old Testament describes this process of taking the darkness they lived with as a cloud of fire that existed over the heads of the Israelites as they walked through the desert for 40 years. The assumption was that the Israelites will learn to love with again and over time nature would transfer these issues to them. When Moses' plan was established it was assumed that his love would last. Moses loss of love for the Israelites created chaos for future generations. The healing event just did not happen. The release of these four winds was going to happen over time but they were not capable of loving so they would only create the darker realities that are chronicled in the Bibles Old Testament.

Later in the prophecy you will read about seven angels with seven trumpets. They sound their trumpets as these issues are released into future generations. The sixth trumpet summarized the events that occurred from the days of Moses until the coming of Jesus. When the sixth trumpet sounds these four winds are released.

> *"And after this I saw four angels standing on the four corners of the earth, holding the four winds of the earth, that the wind should not blow on the earth nor on the sea nor on any tree. And I saw another angel ascending from the rising of the sun, having the seal of the living God; and he cried with a loud voice to the four angels to whom it was given to hurt the earth and the sea, saying: Hurt not the earth nor the sea nor the trees, till we shall have sealed the servants of our God on their foreheads."* (REV. 7:1 – 7:3)

THE BOOK WITH SEVEN SEALS

The prophecy is using this book to say several things.

Through the unconditional love that Moses demonstrated for the Israelites these seven seals were released from the book of knowledge of love and light and it opened mankind's potential to create. When Moses lost his love for the Israelites the love that was needed so people could evolve into a light based spirit was missing from creation. Jesus came and this reality changed. Today, individually we are still learning to create a spirit that is capable of reading from the book of knowledge of love and light and then use what we learn in our day to day lives to create a forgiving spirit throughout the world. As we learn to love again we are releasing these seals that seal us individually.

As we learn to forgive and love collectively we create an even more powerful potential to make this world a better place. To forgive collectively means large groups of people have to learn to forgive one another for things that happened in their past. When nations founded on religious and spiritual beliefs like Islam and Israel learn to forgive one another we will begin the process of healing collectively. Nations like America and Russia; Afghanistan, Iraq, and Iran; Korea and Japan all have to learn to forgive what happened in the past and learn to love one another again. These are only a few of the examples that apply to the global healing we all have to lead. We have to be the leaders of this forgiveness. We cannot rely on political leaders or leaders of any other part of our societies to do what only we can do.

The process of healing requires that a person (people) be broken down completely and then the process of healing can begin. This is the moral of the story of the prodigal son. When we reach that point in our life when we accept that the hurtful things we do are not acceptable and we feel remorse for what we did to others and to ourselves we are ready to begin the quest to find our light.

The next chapter in the prophecy talks about 144,000 Israelites that are sealed. There are 12 tribes and 12,000 members in each tribe. Then the prophecy talks about many people that will be sealed. The prophecy is saying that the Israelites were sealed and that everyone else was going to be sealed. It makes this statement because the original plan identified them as being sealed by the Egyptians and then Moses was going to help.

But, Moses was not able to maintain his light and this reality prevented the Israelites from evolving into a better way of life. Since the seals were released from the book and the powers of creation became a reality to mankind. All of mankind was going to create in the same way as the Israelites. In other words the darkness that was perpetuated by the Israelites and others that lived in the Middle East was going to spread throughout the world. As future generations experienced life with this reality of creation the darkness that nature was going to hold for all of us was much greater than originally planned.

After the statement about the 144,000 that were sealed, the prophecy describes the collective spirit of mankind as people from, "... every nation and the tribes and peoples and tongues" (Rev. 7.9). This is also describing the structure of the collective spirit of mankind. Nations were made up of tribes and people that were committed to the spirit of the nation and their tribes.

The seventh seal states that there was silence in heaven for half an hour and then seven angels with seven trumpets are seen. One hour would represent the time needed for this part of the plan to be completed. Since the plan was not completed only half an hour is presented in the prophecy because half the plan was completed.

THE SEVEN ANGELS WITH SEVEN TRUMPETS

This part of the story is about the follow-up to the plan that was started in the days of Moses. Moses demonstrated unconditional love that released the seals from the book of seven seals and the power of creation was released into the family of the Israelites and into the world. The plan was for Moses to teach the younger generation of Israelites how to cleanse their spirits and learn to live with light again. Then the darkness that was created from their life in Egypt would be cleansed from their spirits and they could live life with a healthy spirit again. The problem with the plan was that Moses did not complete his part of the plan. Before he was able to have the time to teach the younger generation of Israelites how to cleanse their spirits he was over thrown by the rest of the Israelites and left to die in the desert. This led to the Israelites living their lives without the opportunity to create through love and light. This is why the Old Testament tells a story of aggression, conflict, war and attempts to commit genocide. Since the collective spirit of the Israelites only perpetuated the darkness of their collective spirit they could only act in this way. Prior to their life in Egypt they did not engage in the wars that existed in the Middle East because their collective spirit was in a much lighter reality than those that were at war. While the Israelites walked through the desert for 40 years it is written that clouds of fire were seen above their heads. This cloud of fire was the anger and rage of their lives that was being transferred out of their spirit and into nature. Nature was holding this darkness until future generations are ready to deal with the issues that caused it. According to the original plan nature would hold this darkness and then feed it back to the future generations so they could deal with the darkness of this life time. If they had to deal with it in a life time after the collective spirit of the Israelites was cleansed it would be much easier to get past these issues that would be considered past life issues. But since Moses was not able to teach the younger generation how to live in light; when the spirit of this fire returned into their lives it only created an even darker and less healthy collective spirit for the Israelites.

The prophecy explains how nature agreed to the plan when Moses opened the book with seven seals by the statement,

"And I saw, and I heard the voice of many angels round about the throne and the living creatures and the elders, and the number of them was myriads of myriads and thousands of thousands. saying with a loud voice: Worthy is the Lamb that was slain to receive power, and riches, and wisdom, and strength, and honor, and glory, and blessing. And every created thing that is in heaven, and those that are on the earth, and under the earth, and in the sea, even those in them, all did I hear saying: To him that sits on the throne and to the Lamb be blessing, and honor, and glory, and might, from age to age. And the four living creatures heard I saying: Amen; and the elders fell down and worshipped." (Rev.5:6 – 5:14)

In the first scene there were seven churches with an angel in each church. In this second scene these angels come out of their church and holding trumpets and then sound their trumpets. The angels in the churches represented seven states of mind that the Israelites and the collective spirit of mankind existed in when we lived in a darker reality. When these trumpets sound the Israelites and the collective spirit of mankind were trying to use the processes of creation to come out of the darkness of these churches but it did not work. Throughout the prophecy these seven angels represent the collective spirit of the Israelites and mankind as we evolve through creation. They represent the history of the collective spirit of mankind and how the creation works to create through our thoughts, words and actions. Therefore it is also the healing process that we will all experience as we re-create the collective spirit of mankind as we evolve through creation.

This part of the prophecy talks about seven angels with seven trumpets. When the angels sound their trumpets fire comes from heaven and is thrown into the earth, the seas, rivers and streams and the sun, moon and stars. This is the same fire that was seen as a cloud of fire over their heads as they marched through the desert for 40 years. Then when the fifth and sixth trumpets are sounded plagues are seen hurting people. Then in the third scene there are seven angels filled with seven plagues holding seven cups. The fire from the cloud of fire that continued coming into the spirit of the Israelites generation after generation and life time after life time is the fire that comes after the trumpets are sounded. Since Moses was not able to teach them how to cleanse their spirits they merely created their collective spirits in an unhealthy way – therefore filled with plagues. The scene with seven angels filled with plagues represents the collective spirit of the Israelites and mankind after Jesus left. It represents the depth of darkness that existed in the collective spirit of mankind and in the air around us; the ambient spirit that was created since the days of Moses.

Each of the first four angels with a trumpet, sound their trumpets and fire is seen and then blood. This part of the prophecy is about what happened after the seals were released and then what happened after Jesus left. The blood is the blood of life that was planted in the collective spirit of the Israelites and mankind after Jesus died.

These first four angels with trumpets refer to the third part of nature that is seen as being destroyed or hurt in some way. We are all connected to nature and nature to us. Nature is connected to us through seven parts of the son of man discussed earlier in the prophecy. It is like a matrix where our creations (the combination of our emotions and feelings plus our thoughts, words and actions) create a spiritual reality in nature. As we learn to love nature and others nature reacts in the same way. As we grow into a more caring collective spirit we will impact the spirit of nature in the same way; animals will become less aggressive and tamer as we become less aggressive and tame these wild horses (the four horsemen) from within us.

Another aspect of these seven angels with seven trumpets is that they represent the repent part of the process of creation more commonly referred to as repent and overcome (forgive and live with love). As people tried to deal with their issues in life they were able to forgive and find some relief from the anger they lived with but were not able to create a spirit capable of holding light. This is the root of the problem with the reality that existed when Moses' plan did not go according to plan. Remember the first reality of creation is "In order to create light you must first live in light". When Moses lost his love for the Israelites this light went out.

"And the first sounded; and there was hail and fire mingled with blood, and it was thrown into the earth; and the third part of the earth was burned up, and the third part of the trees was burned up, and all green grass was burned up." (Rev. 8.7)

After the time of Moses the plan of creation worked as the collective spirit of the Israelites continued to create more of the anger-based reality that was a reflection of who they were. The fire that was created from their 40 year march in the desert was held by nature and over time nature did its part in the original plan and returned the rage-based spirit into the collective spirit of the Israelites. Since the Israelites were not able to transform their spirit into light they could only perpetuate the darkness of their spiritual reality. Nature continued to hold onto more of this darkness. The prophecy illustrated this as the third part of the earth as being burned up. Fire also lights the way for the Jesus to be able to see where the problem is; as he worked to fix the problem.

The fire from this trumpet represents the rage the Israelites lived with while walking through the desert for 40 years. It also represents any and all rage created throughout the existence of mankind that is stored in the earth until future generations are able to cleanse it form the realities of their lives.

After Jesus came and fixed the plan his spirit was the seed that was planted into the collective spirit of mankind and nature naturally became filled with the blood of his spirit. This blood is the blood of life. The blood of life and how it works through creation will be explained in greater detail later in this book. This reality of the life of Jesus affects each of the first three trumpets in a similar way.

THE ANGEL WITH THE SECOND TRUMPET, EVOLVED FROM THE SECOND CHURCH

"And the second angel sounded; and as it were a great mountain burning with fire was cast into the sea; and the third part of the sea became blood, and the third part of the creatures that were in the sea, that had life, died, and the third part of the ships were destroyed." (Rev. 8.9)

The fire from the mountain is about the repeated attempts for nature to return these issues related to love of self to the Israelites. Since they were not able to get past their issues in life and use the process of creating light in their spirit; this reality of creation made more darkness. Generation after generation and lifetime after lifetime they collected more issues and hatred for this part of nature to hold for them. They turned into a mountain of issues and fire that someday will need to be resolved. This mountain of issues is also the cumulative effects of all the hatred created throughout the world by all of mankind. For the past two thousand years we have been dealing with these issues and are finally are just beginning to create some light in a world that is still filled with darkness.

Soon there will be a generation that will begin to transform this lustful reality and the spirit of it from our existence. As we learn to create love not just make love by having sex we will begin to transform the spirit of lust from our lives.

THE ANGEL WITH THE THIRD TRUMPET, EVOLVED FROM THE THIRD CHURCH

"and there fell from heaven a great star burning as a lamp, and it fell upon the third part of the rivers and upon the fountains of waters. And the name of the star is called Wormwood. And the third part of the waters became wormwood, and many men died of the waters, because they were made bitter." (Rev. 8.11)

Greed grows from a lack of love of others especially family and close friends. The issues related to this star burning as a lamp related to the greed based behaviors that existed in the lives of the Israelites. These rivers and streams turned bitter because there was bitterness in the lives of the Israelites. While they were not perfect in their lives, others in the Middle East were no different than they were. The Israelites merely stood up to their bully and were condemned to a life of misery because of it. They were tricked by an Egyptian and then abused by the very people that offered them the chance to have a better life. This bitterness stayed with them for many lifetimes. As they lived with bitterness in their thoughts, words and actions they created more of it throughout their lives. It became so overpowering that it literally poisoned many of them as they died of this poison within their spirit.

You have to understand that this poison lived in the collective spirit of the Israelites and still exists between the spirit of Israel and Islam. Until we all grow past the sins of the past and learn to forgive one another; this bitterness will continue to plague all of mankind.

When this angel sounded its trumpet it lit a bright light on the root cause of the problem. The third part of man is in reference to the loss of love of family. It was the greed of the second church and third seal that replaced love of others especially family and close friends. When the Israelites turned on Moses and he lost his love for them, they created this reality within their collective spirit.

This is why the third part of nature and the third part of man is referenced as being destroyed throughout the prophecy. The lack of love of family that destroyed the spirit of Moses created a very bad reality in their lives, in their collective spirit and their soul's consciousness. A lack of love of family is prevalent in the creation of this darker reality that still exists in all our lives. The Bible starts this process of lack of love of family with Adam and Eve's two children, Cain and Abel.

As you may know Cain became envious of his brother Abel and killed him.

Later in the stories of the Bible the leader of the Israelites had to send the mother of his first born child and his son into the desert to begin their lives alone.

The next generation of children born to the leader of the Israelites, Isaac, had twin sons, Esau and Jacob. Isaac was old and blind when he wanted to bless his son Esau so Esau would become the leader of the Israelites. Isaac's wife disagreed with his decision to pass the family blessing and leadership of the family onto Esau. She encouraged Jacob to trick Isaac into blessing him as the leader of the family. Since they were twins Jacob convinced his blind father that he was his brother and received the blessing.

Then it was Jacob's sons that turned on their brother Joseph and almost killed him. Instead of killing him they sold him to some merchants that eventually sold him to some guards that worked for the pharaoh of Egypt. Joseph became a slave for the pharaoh and many years later interpreted a dream for the pharaoh that made the pharaoh the ruler of all of the Middle East nations. As the story continues the Jacob learns that Joseph is in Egypt and wants him to return home. The pharaoh does not want to love this man that created all his power so the pharaoh offers Jacob the best land in Egypt if he moves his family to Egypt. Then, after this pharaoh dies his son rules the land and abuses the Israelites in a very aggressive way and destroys their spirits.

Then Moses leads them out of Egypt. If he had loved them completely and they had not lost his love for them he would have changed the collective spirit of the Israelites forever. But since he was not able to hold his love and light for them, their collective spirit was doomed to be sealed into the darkness of their reality until the days of Jesus.

Until love of family exists in their collective spirit they were going to be destined to live with a very hurtful reality. The problem grew even bigger as the spirit of the Middle East was spreading all around the world. It was spreading the same illnesses in their collective spirit to Europe and other lands. Of course the Israelites were not the only people in the world that lived with this reality in their collective spirit. Today we all know that we are one family and connected in spirit to one another. It has taken mankind several thousand years of learning to repent and overcome to begin to recognize this reality as we are just beginning to forgive one another and live with love again.

THE ANGEL WITH THE FOURTH TRUMPET, EVOLVED FROM THE FOURTH CHURCH

And the fourth angel sounded; and the third part of the sun was smitten, and the third part of the moon, and the third part of the stars, that the third part of them might be darkened, and the day might not shine for the third part of it, and the night likewise. (Rev. 8:12)

As the Israelites lived for about 1,700 years with a lack of compassion for those that wished them harm they lived in the fear that now waits in the heavenly bodies hoping to someday return to them.

This darkness impacted nature in such a way as to smite the third part of the sun, moon and stars. The phrase, "the day might not shine and the third part of it and the night likewise" is in reference to the creation of night and day from the book of Genesis. The third part of night and the third part of day are opposite sides of the kingdom of the heavens that relate to love of family and close friends.

All of these four trumpets are simply describing the reality of mankind being sealed into a darker reality and its effect on nature. The first three relate to what mankind created through greed, lust and gluttony; this fourth merely holds the fear that is the foundation on which the anger hatred and rage which are the foundations of greed, lust and gluttony. Fear is the foundation on which all of the darker realities are built.

The next phrase is a warning about what was coming in their lives as they continued to live and create while sealed in this darker reality.

> *"And I saw, and heard an eagle flying in the midst of heaven, saying with a loud voice: Woe, woe, woe to them that dwell on the earth because of the rest of the voices of the trumpet of the three angels that are about to sound."* (Rev. 8:13)

The significance of this statement is that the forces of creation were released not only for the Israelites but for all of mankind. As Moses' plan did not work, all of mankind was able to create through these forces of creation. Collectively we were not any different from the Israelites. Therefore the amount of darkness that was going to be created was much greater than originally planned and nature continued to hold it for all of us.

THE ANGEL WITH THE FIFTH TRUMPET, EVOLVED FROM THE FIFTH CHURCH

> *And the fifth angel sounded: and I saw a star that had fallen from heaven to the earth, and to him was given the key of the pit of the abyss. And he opened the pit of the abyss; and there arose out of the pit a smoke as the smoke of a great furnace, and the sun and the air were darkened by means of the smoke of the pit. And out of the smoke came forth locusts upon the earth, and to them was given power as the scorpions of the earth have power. And it was said to them that they should not hurt the grass of the earth, neither any green thing nor any tree, but the men such as have not the seal of God in their foreheads. And it was given to them that they should not kill them, but that they should be tormented five months; and this torment is as the torment of a scorpion, when he strikes a man. And in those days men shall seek death and shall not find it, and they shall desire to die and death flees from them. And the shape of the locusts was like horses prepared for battle, and on their heads as crowns like gold, and; their faces as the faces of men. and they had hair as the hair of women, and their teeth were as the teeth of lions, and they had breastplates as breastplates of iron, and the sound of their wings as the sound of chariots of many horses running to battle. And they have tails like scorpions, and stings, and in their tails is their power to hurt men five months: they have a king over them, the angel of the abyss, his name in Hebrew is Abaddon, but in Greek he has the name Apollyon. The first woe has past: behold, there come two woes more after this.* (Rev. 9:1 – 9:12)

The warring competitive conflict driven nature of mankind at this time in our history created through the spirit of the four horsemen. The judgmental and vengeful nature of mankind perpetuated their existence in our spirits and souls. The spirit of mankind was not healthy and over time it became plagued because of the results of its efforts. Revelations refers to this as their labor and their works.

HOW WE CREATE AN ASPECT OF OUR LIFE IN OUR SPIRIT - LIVING WITH JUDGMENT IS ABOUT

When you judge others in your life your spirit becomes one with the spirit of all others that have judging spirits. It is like there is a pool of people that all have the same spirit as yourself. The first time you judge someone it is like wading into the shallow end of the pool. You test the waters to see if feels OK to be there; to be in that state of mind. It is like when you first feel fear of someone you might judge them and then the fear will go away. Then as time goes on you will have to choose to continue to judge others or to stop. Most people do not feel very bad after the first time they judge someone and the feeling of judging them did make him or her feel better so they do it again. As fears in your life grow you take that next step into the pool of judgment. As you wade farther into this pool the less aware you will become of the reality that existed when you did not judge others. You lose your connection to love and light as your spirit now goes to sleep while you swim with the spirits of others. This process of wading deeper into the pool continues until you learn to swim with the rest of the peoples' spirits that judge others. Then as you continue to judge others and your spirit becomes immersed in the spirit of this pool of judgment you will feel as if you are being judged. It is only natural that this will happen because your spirit has become one with all the others that are now a part of your collective consciousness. Now, the more you feel judged, the more you will judge others. This is what it is like to be judged by the jury of your fears.

ENTERING THE PIT OF THE ABYSS – LOSING THE EMOTIONS THAT USED TO GUIDE YOUR ACTIONS

The pit of the abyss is about living with no feelings or emotional content at all. To create with no love is to create through ire, distain and wrath of the abyss. When mankind lived with this reality of nature in their lives they could only create more of that which they were. We created and released the scorpions that are referred to in the above quote from the prophecy. We were literally destroying our own collective spirit from within. Once the process of creation was released and we did not know how to live with the power of it in our lives; plus the fact that we were all sealed in this darkness we were doomed to live this way until Jesus came to help. As discussed earlier we were sealed into this reality because there was no love in the collective spirit of mankind to help us evolve into a better reality. The first reality of creation is, "in order to create light we must first live in light".

THE ANGEL WITH THE SIXTH TRUMPET, EVOLVED FROM THE SIXTH CHURCH

This sixth angel with a trumpet explains several things:

1) What happens when people try to learn to love again
2) The powers that be in creation measure the progress the Israelites have made toward healing from the effects of living with the Egyptians.
3) The problem that existed because Moses was not able to teach the younger generation of Israelites how to re-create their collective spirit.
4) Then talks about the coming of Jesus.

There were problems experienced by the Israelites and mankind throughout the 1,700 years they were struggling to learn to live with a greater power to create and learning to love again.

THE FOUR ANGELS WITH THE FOUR WINDS ARE RELEASED

Earlier in the prophecy there were four angels that were told to hold the four winds until the time was right to release them. These four winds are the four loves that were lost when the Israelites collective spirits were sealed into a darker reality.

> *"And the sixth angel sounded; and I heard a voice from the four horns of the golden altar that is before God, saying to the sixth angel, that had the trumpet: Loose the four angels that are bound on the great river Euphrates. And the four angels were loosed, who were prepared for an hour and a day and a month and a year, to slay the third part of men."* *(REV 9:13 – 9:15)*

The sounding of this trumpet releases these loves into mankind's existence but we were not ready to receive them. Our spirits were not strong enough to hold the light that comes with them. This created a lot of chaos in their lives. The Bible's Old Testament documented the history of the Israelites when their spirits were not capable of holding light. The third part of man is that part of their spirits that were slayed since the days the Israelites lived with the Egyptians.

The prophecy goes on to describe the lack of healing that existed in their spirits at this point in time. This is what the Israelites and mankind still needed to do to cleanse their spirits.

> *"And the rest of men, that were not killed by these plagues, repented not of the works of their hands, that they should not worship demons and idols of gold and of silver and of brass and of stone and of wood, which can neither see, nor hear, nor walk, and they repented not of their murders, neither of their sorceries nor of their lewdness nor of their thefts."* (REV. 9:20 – 9:21)

"And I saw another angel that was mighty descending from heaven, clothed with a cloud, and a rainbow was upon his head, and Ins face was as the sun, and his feet as pillars of fire; and he had in his hand a little book opened. And he put his right foot on the sea, but his left on the land, and he cried with a loud voice as a lion roars. And when he had cried, the seven thunders uttered their voices. And when the seven thunders had spoken, I was about to write; and I heard a voice from heaven, saying: Seal up the things that the seven thunders spoke, and write them not. And the angel that I saw standing on the sea and on the earth, lifted up his right hand to heaven. and swore by him that lives from age to age, who created the heaven and the things that are in it, and the earth and the things that are in it, and the sea and the things that are in it, that time should no longer be, but in the days of the voice of the seventh angel, when he shall sound, and the mystery of God was finished, as he proclaimed to his servants the prophets. And the voice that I heard from heaven again spoke to me and said: Go, take the little book that is opened in the hand of the angel that stands on the sea and on the earth. And I went to the angel, saying to him that he should give me the little book. And he said to me: Take it and eat it up, and it will make thy belly bitter, but in thy mouth it shall be sweet as honey. And I took the little book out of the hand of the angel and ate it up; and it was in my mouth as honey, sweet; and when I had eaten it, my belly was bitter. And they say to me: Thou must again prophesy against many peoples and nations and tongues and kings. (Rev. 10:1 – 10:11)

The image of an angel coming down from heaven with a little book that is open represents the plan not going according to plan. It means the book that was sealed by seven seals is open but only a few people have been able to evolve and the evolution was small; only a little higher consciousness had entered mankind's consciousness. St. John is asked to eat the book and it tastes sweet in his mouth but turns bitter in his stomach; this is because the process of creation that is supposed to re-create a person's spirit was too hard and not working. People were not able to forgive and love; therefore they were not able to evolve into a better reality. They were stuck and needed help. The bitterness of the process as well as the bitterness of the spirit of the Israelites is what he tasted.

This image of an angel standing on both the land and the water means that the spirit of creation had impacted more than just the Israelites and it was first planned. It also spread overseas to other nations like the Roman Empire.

The next chapter is about St. John being given a reed to measure the temple of God and all those that worship in it. In this chapter he is being shown that the collective spirit of mankind was being measured to see what the problem is and where it exists in evolution. He is asked to measure the court that is without the temple for it is given to the Gentiles and the holy city will be tread down for forty-two months. This is the kingdom of the heavens and he is measuring how much of it, the collective spirit had evolved into it.

He is being asked to measure only the dark and the light of the heavens not the part that is the transition from dark to light. The 40-2 months represents the part of the kingdom of the heavens that is the 4 loves (40) and the lesser and greater lights (2) of this transition area. The only information that was needed to determine if the plan was working was to know if mankind's spirit had evolved into the light of day.

Something was missing and someone had to come and fix it. This is when Jesus was born. The prophecy then says.

> "And I will give to my two witnesses, and they shall prophesy a thousand two hundred and sixty days, clothed in sackcloth. These are the two olive-trees and the two candlesticks that stand before the Lord of the earth." (Rev. 11:3- 11.4)

The two olive trees are the seeds of forgiveness and living with love that Jesus will plant in the collective spirit of mankind. The two candlesticks are wrath and gluttony. Forgiveness and living with love were the seeds that had to be planted so mankind could repent and overcome the spirit of gluttony and the anger, hatred and rage of the church of wrath. If you remember from reading the riddle of the first scene the candlesticks are the churches. This is because the spirit of mankind fills the churches which are the spirit of man; therefore the collective spirit of mankind exists in the candlesticks which are in the kingdom of the heavens. In this way the candle sticks are the churches and the churches are the candlesticks.

The reality of the spirit of wrath (church of Ephesus) is that it is the fear, anger, hatred, rage, ire, distain and wrath that combine with the essence of greed, lust, gluttony, sloth, pride and envy to make the spirit of these seven deadly sins. This part of the prophecy is about creating something in the collective spirit of mankind that would allow mankind to evolve beyond the darkness of its spiritual existence. The part of the heavens that Jesus had to create was the gray area of the lesser light and greater light of the heavens. There are two sides and four sections (or churches) we have to grow beyond. Then, over time, mankind could evolve through this gray area and into the light. This was the problem that existed 2,000 years ago when Jesus came to fix the problem. By living with the love and light of a forgiving spirit he planted the seeds of forgiveness and love in the collective spirit of mankind. The planting of these seeds was his purpose. When his purpose was complete he died and the rest was left to the Israelites, mankind, creation and evolution to allow these seeds to grow. They have grown and the two trees (forgiveness and love) have just begun to produce the fruits of our labors. Our collective spirits, in the past 50 – 100 years, have just started to enter this gray area of the heavens. The first part of the gray area that we have to evolve beyond is gluttony. The spirit of gluttony is a combination of cravings (the essence of gluttony) and rage (the emotion of wrath).

> *"And if any one will hurt them, fire comes forth from their mouth and devours their enemies; and if any one will hurt them, they must be put to death. These have authority to shut heaven, that rain fall not in the days of their prophecy, and they have authority over the waters to turn them into blood, and to smite the earth with every plague as often as*

they will. And when they shall have accomplished their testimony, the beast that ascends out of the abyss shall make war with them and overcome them and kill them. And their dead bodies in the street of the great city, which is called, spiritually, Sodom and Egypt, where our Lord also was crucified. And they of the peoples and tribes and tongues and nations see their dead bodies three days and a half, and suffer not their dead bodies to be put into a tomb. And they that dwell on the earth rejoice over them and make merry, and shall send gifts one to another, because these two prophets tormented them that dwell on the earth. And after three days and a half the spirit of life from God entered into them, and they stood upon their feet, and great fear fell upon those that saw them. And I heard a great voice out of heaven saying to them: Come up hither; and they went up into heaven in a cloud, and their enemies beheld them. And in that hour there was a great earthquake, and the tenth part of the city fell, and there were killed in the earthquake names of men seven thousand, and the rest were frightened and gave glory to the God of heaven. The second woe was passed: the third woe, behold, it comes quickly." (Rev. 11:5- 11.14)

This is obviously the story of Jesus and his efforts to bring forgiveness and love into the collective spirit of mankind.

What is pertinent to the prophecy is the number 3 ½. This chapter of the prophecy says that two witnesses will prophesy for 1,260 days which is 3 ½ years and it also says that these two prophets will lay dead in the street for 3 ½ days. In the next chapter there is a reference to 1,260 days in which a woman will hide in a desert and several references to 42 months which also is 3 ½ years.

The number 3 ½ is significant at this point in the prophecy because there are 3 ½ generations in each life time. In the next chapter of this book you will learn that these 3 ½ generations are a very important part of the process of creation and Jesus' plan to heal all of mankind.

THE ANGEL WITH THE 7TH TRUMPET

"And the seventh angel sounded; and there were great voices in heaven, saying: The kingdom of the world has become our Lord's and his Christ's, and he shall reign from age to age. And the twenty-four elders that sat on their thrones before God fell on their faces and worshipped God, saying: We give thee thanks. Lord God, the Almighty who art and who wast, because thou hast taken thy great power and hast reigned; and the nations were angry, and thy wrath has come, and the time of the dead that they should be judged, and that thou shouldst give reward to thy servants the prophets and to thy saints and to those that fear thy name, both small and great, and that thou shouldst destroy those that destroy the earth. And the temple of God was opened in heaven, and there appeared in his temple the ark of his covenant, and there were lightnings, and voices, and thunderings, and an earthquake, and great hail." (Rev. 11:15- 11.19)

When a person's spirit ascends into the heavens his or her spirit evolves into the purest most transparent light and consciousness. The end game for all of us will be when the collective spirit of mankind ascends into heaven.

There was a phrase earlier in the prophecy about saints asking when others would be judged in the same way that they were judged. The phrase, *"and the time of the dead that they should be judged,"* is referring to the firth seal when the saints were praying for the souls of those that still existed with spirits in the abyss. A spirit and soul existing in the abyss is said to be dead to the love and light of creation. In the first scene there is a phrase in each of the churches that says when a person repents and overcomes the issues related to that church, he or she will receive a reward for their efforts; this is what is meant by the phrase, *"and that thou shouldst give reward to thy servants the prophets and to thy saints"*. To *"destroy those that destroy the earth"* simply means that the transformation of a darker spirit into a lighter spirit is similar to destroying the darkness of the collective spirit of mankind and replacing it with light.

This marks the end of the first part of the plan. From this point forward it was up to us to just let creation do its thing. Naturally it has and we are beginning to find our way out of the darkness that existed. But there was more darkness in the collective spirit of mankind and in the Israelites than originally planned for. To give nature, the Israelites and mankind a chance to work through this process some changes were needed. There was a lot of momentum in creation that was not good. People believed in the age old adage "an eye for an eye and a tooth for a tooth" as well anger hatred and rage were nothing compared to the ire, distain and wrath that filled the air. Now the transformation that was needed was more than just the collective spirit of the Israelites. The transformation now included all of mankind and the ambient spirit that mankind had been creating for 1,700 years. The revision to the plan is what we will talk about in the chapter of this book.

This marks the end of the second scene and the end of an era in time or the end of mankind's time spent on our journey into darkness and the beginning of our quest to find light.

CHAPTER 4

THE WOMAN ABOUT TO GIVE BIRTH TO A CHILD AND A DRAGON WITH SEVEN HEADS WAITING TO CONSUME THE CHILD

Mankind's evolution from the time of Jesus through today

1) the woman about to five birth to a child
2) a dragon waiting to consume the child (has seven heads and ten horns)
3) the first beast – the beast of the sea
4) the first beast - beast of the earth
    a. how we created the greed based business and finance systems that exist today
5) the dragon and two beasts summarized
6) and the great winepress
    a. incarnation/reincarnation
7) the seven angels filled with plagues holding seven cups
8) the prophecies message to mankind for this scene
9) the mystery of Babylon

THUS FAR THE PROPHECY HAS GROWN FROM A COMPLETE BEING, ADAM,
THROUGH THE BROKEN SPIRITS OF ADAM AND EVE,
TO THE COLLECTIVE SPIRIT OF MANKIND.

WE HAVE TALKED ABOUT HOW THE COLLECTIVE SPIRIT OF MANKIND AND AN INDIVIDUAL
PERSON'S SPIRIT WORK TOGETHER.

THE EVOLUTION OF THE BROKEN SPIRIT THROUGH CREATION IS A REALITY OF CREATION.

NOW THE PROPHECY INTRODUCES ANOTHER REALITY OF CREATION – THAT WHICH WE CREATE
COLLECTIVELY THROUGH OUR THOUGHTS, WORDS AND ACTIONS – THE AMBIENT SPIRIT OF
MANKIND, BABYLON.

THE AMBIENT SPIRIT OF MANKIND LIVES IN THE AIR AROUND US.

IT IS THE RESULT OF MANY PEOPLE WITH A DEEP PASSIONATE COMMITMENT TO WHAT THEY
SAY, THINK AND DO.

THE SPIRIT OF OUR COLLECTIVE PASSION AND THE THOUGHTS, WORDS AND ACTIONS
ACCOSICATED WITH IT, CREATE THE SPIRIT OF OUR THOUGHTS, WORDS AND ACTIONS.
2,000 YEARS AGO PEOPLE CALLED THIS REALITY OF CREATION THEIR GODS.

THE WOMAN ABOUT TO GIVE BIRTH TO A CHILD

The prophecy says this child will rule all nations with an iron rod.

There is a dragon waiting to consume this child and then a beast that looks similar to the dragon. Finally this scene has another beast with two horns on its head just like a lamb and speaks like a dragon.

This scene of the prophecy explains how one of the most powerful forces in creation works to transform the collective spirit of mankind and heal all of us lifetime after lifetime and generation after generation. This is the revised plan that Jesus set in motion when he planted the seeds of forgiveness and love.

This is the power of generations of children that enter the world lifetime after lifetime.

In every life time there are 3 ½ generations of children that enter the world with a lighter spirit, greater consciousness (conscious awareness) and a purpose to use their spirit and soul's consciousness to change the world.

The prophecy and several parables taught by Jesus explain how great conflict will exist between these generations. This foundation in creation will create a gap in the reality created from one generation to the next. Today we refer to this gap as the generation gap.

> *"A fire came I to throw upon the earth, and what would I if it were already kindled? A baptism have I to be baptized with, and how am I in pain till it be accomplished. Think you that I came to give peace on earth? I tell you no, but rather division. For there shall be, from this time, five in one house divided; three against two and two against three shall they be divided, father against son and son against father; mother against daughter and daughter against mother; mother-in-law against daughter-in-law, and daughter-in-law against mother-in-law."* (Luke 12:49 – 12:53)

> *"Think not that I came to send peace on the earth, I came not to send peace, but a sword. For I came to set a man in opposition to his father, and a daughter to her mother, and a daughter-in-law to her mother-in-law; and a man's enemies shall be those of his household."* (Matthew 10:34 – 10:36)

Thousands of years ago the collective spirit of mankind was structured according to the family, tribe and nation you were born into. It was critical to the survival of these tribes and nations that everyone be one in spirit. It was not about being one with the collective spirit of mankind. The survival of each tribe and nation was a function of its ability to manage the spirit of those within it. This left very little flexibility or opportunity to change. Parents forced their children to do as they were told. Parents taught their children to do as their father taught them to do and their father taught then to do as their grandfather taught them to do. The Bible says, in the days of Jesus, parents were still teaching their children to do as the founding father of the family of the Israelites believed was right. Abraham led the Israelites almost 2,000 years before Jesus was born. The stories in the Bible tell of people that would stone their children in order to prevent them from bringing new thoughts and ideas into a family. In the days of Jesus children were forced to lose their connection to their love and light and the essence of who they were at very young ages. These actions created the suppressive and oppressive spirits that evolved into the Roman Empires strategy to rule the Roman Empire. When a person's spirit is broken his or her willpower is weaker. To live with a weakened spirit is to not be able to protect yourself from another person asserting their will on you. A reality of nature and creation is that people with a weaker spirit strive to force their will on others. It is just a reality in nature that a person with a spirit not capable of holding light will strive to create a broken spirit in others so they can then assert their will on them. This is a big motivation behind the spirit of bullying. This was the reality of the Roman Empire and its leaders.

In the past and still today in many families, parents bully their children in such a way as to break their spirit so children will do as they are told.

In the past and still today governments and empires (like the Roman Empire) strive to destroy the spirit of those in their country so they can rule over them. When the Roman Empire broke the spirit of the people in their empire it made it much easier to manage the empire. Taking the spirit of so many people created another reality that the leaders did not anticipate. It was the absorption of the spirit of those that were being suppressed into the spirit of the leaders of the empire. This is what led to many to the leaders of the empire to be drunk on the power of their role as ruler.

In the past the spirit of bullying was created; and it still exists today. As people are trying to prevent parents, police, teachers and many more from bullying others they are only empowering others to bully those that we have depowered. The spirit of bullying will always exist until:

1) We learn to forgive those that bully us.
2) We all accept the reality that we create the opportunity for the spirit of bullying to be a part of our children's lives when we bully create a weaker spirit within our children.

After Jesus fulfilled his purpose and the seeds of the spirit of forgiveness and love (especially love of family and close friends) were planted in the collective spirit of the Israelites and mankind. His efforts were about to change this reality of hurting children.

Generations of children were about to enter the world with a greater spirit, consciousness and will than had ever entered the world. With this greater light and a purpose to use it they were going to rule over the older generations with an iron rod. There was a strategy coming that would involve three generations that would change the spirit of the world and the reality of the lives of those that live in it. The results of this plan are coming to fruition today.

There are 3 ½ generations per lifetime. Each life time has a spiritual mission to create the changes that are needed. Within each life time there will be a change in the spirit of mankind, the consciousness of mankind and the reality that exists in the world. The first generation brings with it a different collective spirit, the second generation uses this newly created spirit and the consciousness into the world and the third generation uses them to change the world and make it a better place. The spirits of the prayers of a previous lifetime or generation bring the specifics related to the mission of a life time and purpose of a generation.

THE DRAGON WAITING TO CONSUME THE CHILD

This image of a dragon waiting to consume a child is about the reality that existed in the Middle East 2,000 years ago and still today throughout the world. It is about the lifestyle and the spirit of mankind that exists when a generation of children is born into the world. The way of life that exists when children are born into the world is the dragon. The way of life that is created by one generation makes that generation feel comfortable with that which they created; when another generation of children come into the world and are naturally motivated to change it there will be great conflict. Each generation comes in to the world to cleanse another layer of the darker reality that was created in past lives.

> For example, when the Israelites were walking in the desert they created their own set of issues and the darkness that accompanied it; in future lives they will have to cleanse that darkness. As future generations came into the world with the light in their spirit and a purpose to cleanse it they made the world a little better. When the Israelites felt as if their survival relied on the close knit spirit of their families and nation; it is only natural that any change in the spirit of the family and nation would be quite frightening. It was natural for people to resist this kind of change but at the same time we now realize that change is inevitable and can be beneficial.

Generations of people create change. They do the best they can with what they have. Ultimately what they have is the light of their spirit, a greater conscious awareness, consciousness and a foundation from the previous generation that they will change. They will always do the best they can with what they have in their hearts and in their mind. This is how God works through us as we make the world a better place. Then another generation comes into the world with a greater light than that which existed in the spirit of those that still live in what is now the lesser light. Those that live in a lesser light will not feel comfortable in the new world that is being created by a younger generation. It will seem scary to the older generation; as if the younger generation should do things the way the older generation did. This creates a great deal of conflict in the world. This is how the spirit of the generation gap works to create our reality, generation after generation and life time after lifetime.

This dragon also represents the past life issues of a person that is waiting to consume them as they enter the world. To deal with the sins of the past can be an all-consuming reality in a person's life. What we take with us is what or who we are at the time of our death. When a person lives a life and changes who they are they change the spirit of who they are. The prophecy refers to this reality of spiritual transformation with the phrase, "your labor and your works". It is through your labors in every life time you live that your spirit changes as the result of the work you do. When you die you take this transformed spirit with you because it now is you, it is your spirit and soul. More specifically you transform your spirits capability to hold light and then your soul's consciousness changes with it.

This dragon can be summarized as three realities:

1) The life style and the spirit of that life style that exists when a child is born into the world.
2) The spirit of the sins of the past that continue to plague the earth with its existence.
3) The past life issues that a person still has to deal with in order to fully cleanse his or her spirit of the sins of the past.

THE FIRST BEAST – THE BEAST OF THE SEA

This beast represents the life of this generation of people that lives to transform the world into a way of life that is in line with their collective purpose in life.

The dragon and this beast both have seven heads and ten horns. The seven heads are the seven parts of one side of the kingdom of the heavens and the ten horns are two sides of the kingdom of the heavens. The ten horns represent the potential for mankind to evolve into both the light and cark of the heavens. The seven heads represented the seven parts of the collective spirit that only existed in the darker side of the heavens; this was at the time of the prophecy shortly after Jesus died.

If you remember the kingdom of the heavens has two sides the dark of night and the light of day that is separated by the firmament. Each side has seven sections. There is also a firmament that separates the dark of night from the light of day. The firmament has four parts to it that are the four loves that we have to learn in order to live with unconditional love again. It is by learning to forgive and live with love (repent and overcome) that we learn to live with the love that comes from this light side of the heavens. When we learn to love there is no longer a need for the firmament. When we live with love and light the seals are released and there is no longer a need for the firmament (greater light and lesser light). To live in the light free of the seals that used to seal our fate we can choose to act in on anger or love. It is a choice that only exists after these seals are released. When some people live in the bright light of the heavens and in the dark there are ten possible realities that we can live in and create through.

There are four parts of our personal spirit that surround our body and feed us the feelings we live with and create through, throughout our lives. Then there are the three parts that connect our spirit to our soul as our soul feeds us the consciousness and knowledge we need in order to function in our lives. These seven heads also represent these seven parts of an individual person and the issues that we live with and have to cleanse in our life time. Each of these parts of our spirit is filled with a set of issues we have to live with and cleanse from our spirit. We enter the world as part of a plan to transform this reality. Each of these heads is the set of issues we are going to deal with.

These seven heads represent how the collective spirit of mankind has evolved from the time of Moses up to the time of Jesus. It is this reality that is the result of the creation that occurred after Moses released the seals. The ten horns represent the expansion of the kingdom of the heavens after Jesus accomplished his purpose. It is mankind's potential to live in either the dark or the light; but first we have to do the work needed to create a place in the light and bright for our collective spirit. It also tells us what is in store for us when we get to the point where we have created a fully functioning collective spirit that fills the kingdom of the heavens completely. When we are capable of living with a full range and depth of emotions we will have created the heavens completely. When this is done there will no longer be a need for the firmament. The firmament is only needed when we experience life without the ability to forgive. The firmament is then needed because we create the seals that seal our fate in a darker reality in life. The process of creation that utilizes generations of children to transform the collective spirit of mankind into this brighter light of the heavens will eventually create the reality that is these ten horns.

One of the heads of this beast is seen as being wounded. This represents the spirit of mankind that existed when these children first entered this world. They entered with a purpose to transform the spirit of one of the seven parts of the collective spirit of mankind. As the people of this generation strive to deal with the issues that have consumed them, the head of this beast is wounded. The wounded head is also seen as healed; this means that the generation was not able to deal with the issues of that life time and cleanse the collective spirit completely. This means that future generations will have to continue to work to transform this darkness into light. The collective spirit and soul change as a result of the lives of this generation. Initially it brings in a greater spirit and then a higher consciousness follows.

Another way to understand how the beast of the sea and the beast of the earth are the generation gap is to realize that while the younger generations (beast of the sea) strive to change the world into a better place it is the older generation (beast of the earth) that strives to keep it the same. As the older generation (the beast of the earth) strives to prevent the changes a younger generation brings into the world the older generation is trying to heal the wound inflicted by the younger generation.

The chart below illustrates how the seven parts of the dark side of the heavens and the seven parts of the light side of the heavens overlap one another to make the ten parts of the heavens (these seven heads and ten horns).

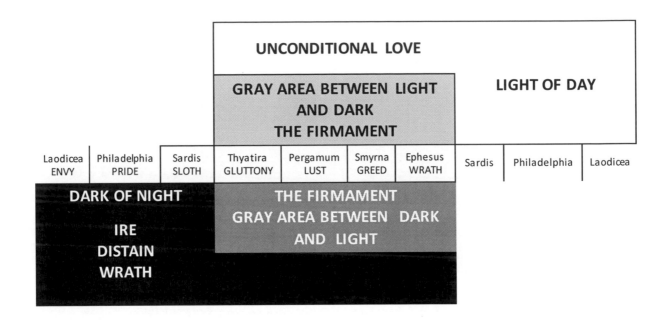

As you can see the ten horns are the kingdom of the heavens when mankind experiences the complete range of emotions that we are capable of feeling.

This generation builds on the spirit of the first generation that came into the world as a part of the mission for this lifetime. They bring with them an emphasis to bring a greater consciousness into the world. They build on the fresh spirit from the previous generation as they live to feel and know what to do especially if it is different from that which exists currently.

THE SECOND BEAST - THE BEAST OF THE EARTH

This beast represents the third of three generations that have a purpose to change the world. They come into the world with a purpose to create a new reality. They build on the foundations of the previous two generations. As they build on the greater spirit and higher consciousness of the previous two generations the have what it takes to change the world.

As one life time and its three generations changes the way of life that existed; it is now creating a way of life that will need to be changed in the future. It actually becomes the dragon that will consume the next set of 3 1/2 generations that will come into the world with another purpose to transform another level of the darkness that exists in our collective spirit.

The way of life that was created before and during the days of the Roman Empire was a money based society that created the gluttonous greed based spirit of business and finance that exists today. It is the greedy spirit of business that is shrinking with the evolution of our collective spirit. As we learn to make transactions through the spirit of being grateful and generous we will transform this greedy nature of business and finance into something more positive.

HOW WE CREATED THE GREED BASED BUSINESS AND FINANCE SYSTEMS THAT EXIST TODAY

When we have an intention to do something our spirit fills with the light of dark of that intention. Our spirit then feeds our body a feeling and we are motivated to act on these feelings. Our soul will then guide our actions as we accomplish our original intention. This is how we work in body, spirit and soul. When we have a very deep emotional moment and are committed to what we are saying or doing we create the spirit of these words and actions. When we share an emotion with someone else we co-create between us the spirit of these words and actions. Co-creating is a very more powerful reality in creation. It gets more powerful as more people are saying and doing the same thing. This is how we create the spirit of our purpose.

When a person is filled with purpose his or her spirit vibrates at its highest levels. This is a very powerful force in attraction. A person with great purpose in his or her life will attract to them what is needed to accomplish their purpose. The more people that get involved with this persons purpose the greater their force in creation. This is why the Roman Empire created a system of trade as the primary activity that people were going to do in order to survive while under their control.

When the leaders of Rome began the strategy they used to manage the people of their Empire the people of the empire were so suppressed by their armies that their spirits were broken. As people had to buy and sell to survive it was only natural that they would create from a lower vibrating reality. It was their fear based need to survive that left them with the only thing they could create through and that was greed.

These beasts are the collective spirit of mankind. The belly of this beast was filled with all the worst things that mankind could create. It is filled with the gluttonous reality of lust and greed as people of that time period created a reality filled with sloth, pride and envy. This is what we have been working towards changing for 2,000 years and we are finally just beginning to transform the belly of this beast into a more positive reality in our lives.

As we are now collectively learning to live with greater emotions than we did for the past two millenniums we are faced with new challenges. To live with emotions makes us much more sensitive to the hurt that others feel. When we do something hurtful to others we feel their hurt and then try to act in a more appropriate way. When we sense or feel that someone else is doing something hurtful to others we try to make them stop doing things that are hurtful to others. Our sensitivity to others means that we are in a better place than we used to be but we are not yet done with our quest to create a light based reality in our lives. As we learn to <u>forgive</u> others for doing hurtful things to us and to others and learn to <u>accept</u> others for who they are we will learn to create more tolerance for the actions of others. This is how to live in a brighter light than just the love that comes with forgiveness.

When one person says or does something that hurts another person's feelings quite often it might be that the person whose feelings are being hurt is the result of a spirit that is still on the mend. To make everyone stop doing the things that might hurt someone because someone has a trigger point in their life will only paralyze everyone and stunt our collective growth. When we try to help those whose feelings are being hurt by someone else's words or actions we can make this world a better place. But trying to stop everyone from saying or doing things because it might hurt someone's feelings will not be very productive emotionally. It is only when a person asks for help, that he or she might be ready to begin his quest.

Of course when someone intentionally tries to say or do something hurtful to others we should intervene and try to make these bullying actions stop. I hope you understand that it is the intention behind someone's words and actions that will create a hurtful or healing spirit as we co-create our new reality.

Transforming the reality of the greed, lust envy and more is what the spirit of this second beast is all about. It talks about three sixes and the number of the beast. This third generation acts on the new feelings and consciousness brought into the world by previous generations. It is these actions that are transformative in nature. They transform the collective spirit and then the ambient spirit that exists throughout the world.

The number 666 is actually 600 and 60-6.

The image of the beast is the number of a man.

These three sixes have several meanings:

1) The explain how creation works collectively
2) They explain how three generations exist in the collective spirit of mankind
3) They explain how the dragon and two beasts were created throughout mankind's existence and how this is explained through the sixth Church, Seal and angel with a trumpet.

HOW THE THREE SIXES EXPLAIN HOW CREATION WORKS COLLECTIVELY

These three sixes relate to the dragon and two beasts. There is a 6 for each of these three images. They are about a reality of creation. When a behavior like buying and selling with a greed based intention exists for more than three generations the spirit of this activity becomes etched in our collective spirits. When a behavior becomes etched in our collective spirit and consciousness it becomes human nature to continue to feed it. This is how we perpetuate the creations of the past. This is why the number 600 and 60-6 is the image of the beast and the sign of a man. It is about how mankind's creation in both the collective spirit of mankind and the ambient spirit of mankind will create a reality in our lives. It is the spirit of all of us that that creates through our thoughts words and actions that creates the spirit that is in air around us. It is this spirit that is in the air all around us and our collective spirit that makes it feel so right to do what we do in life (even if the things we do might be hurtful towards others). The re-creation of the collective spirit leads to the re-creation of the ambient spirit of mankind. As we change our personal spirits we change the collective spirit. As we change the collective spirit we transform the ambient spirit that has existed for thousands of years. This is how we have transformed the spirit of the Greek gods and Roman gods into the spirit of business and finance systems.

HOW THE THREE SIXES EXPLAIN THE THREE GENERATIONS THAT EXIST IN THE COLLECTIVE SPIRIT OF MANKIND

There are 3 ½ generation that exist in every life time (children, parents and grandparents). The numbers 600 and 60 and 6 indicate:

1) The youngest generation (ages 0 – 2) that is creating a new higher vibrating spirit as they enter the world. These are the 600 because they have a higher vibrating spirit.
2) The next generation (ages 22 – 44) that is creating changes throughout the world as their spirit and purpose is manifesting a new reality in the world. These are the 60 because theirs is the next highest vibrating spirit.
3) The older generation that has already completed their purpose and are trying to live comfortably in the world they created while the younger generations are trying to make it a better place for themselves. These are the 6. These are the 6 because theirs are the lowest vibrating spirit respectively.

They each receive power from the previous generation and they have to learn to feed off what existed while simultaneously re-create what exists into what they need in order to feed their personal and collective spirits. Each generation is consumed by the collective spirit that that exists as part of the reality of life. Children are consumed by the spirit of their parents and the family they live in. These children will eventually grow up and be motivated to change the world and make it a better place for their spirit(s).

HOW THE THREE SIXES EXPLAIN HOW THE DRAGON AND TWO BEASTS WERE CREATED THROUGHOUT MANKIND'S EXISTENCE AND HOW THIS IS EXPLAINED THROUGH THE SIXTH CHURCH, SEAL AND ANGEL WITH A TRUMPET.

The seven churches with an angel in each church, seven seals and seven trumpets are the collective spirit of mankind and explain how we evolve throughout time. They explain the seven parts of the kingdom of the heavens that were created by mankind throughout time and they explain the state of mind and state of spirit that existed at each time in the history of mankind. These three times are the beginning (Genesis), the first attempt at creation (Exodus and the Old Testament) and the beginning of the third time when Jesus came to help (the New Testament). There is something unique about the sixth church with an angel, sixth seal and sixth angel with a trumpet. They all explain mankind's evolution. The three sixes are one of the keys needed to unlock the secrets of the prophecy. The 6, 6, 6 interpretation relates to the 6th church, 6th, seal and 6th angel with a trumpet. As well there is one 6 for the dragon, one 6 for the beast of the sea and one 6 for the beast of the earth. Throughout the prophecy the 6th church, seal and angel are telling the story of the evolution of mankind's collective spirit and the dragon and two beasts are that which we manifested collectively over time.

Mankind's journey into the reality we created began with the 6th church with an angel in it. It is referred to as the church of Philadelphia. The prophecy describes mankind as hiding in caves waiting for the mountain to fall on us. This is the reality of life filled with fear that existed in the beginning.

Our journey continued and was described as the release of the 6th seal. Here mankind's journey is about to evolve into a new reality; the collective reality. This seal describes the journey of the Israelites into the desert as their collective spirits were destroyed by the Egyptian Pharaoh. It was the pharaoh's jealousy towards the Israelites that motivated him to mistreat them the way he did. He was the Pharaoh's son but Joseph (the Israelite who interpreted the visions that predicted 7 years of prosperity followed by 7 years of famine and drought) was favored over him and then Moses (who was also an Israelite was a favorite son). When the pharaoh passed away and his son became the leader of the Egyptians; his envy motivated him to mistreat the Israelites and eventually Moses led them out of Egypt. The unconditional love demonstrated by Moses released the seals that sealed mankind's fate and our journey into creation began. The seals released our potential to create; what we created is documented in the Bible's Old Testament as war's and conflict that manifested the god's of war, pleasure and others that existed at that time in our history. This was the beginning of the time when mankind learned to rely on a large collective reality in order to survive. This is what the images and symbols of the 6th seal are explaining.

The prophecy continues to describe the evolution of mankind's journey in the part about the 6th angel with a trumpet. This part of the prophecy explains how the plan to bring the power of creation into mankind's life did not go according to plan. Moses was supposed to lead the Israelites until he had a chance to teach the youngest generation that entered the desert was able to learn how to re-create their spirits; but before he was able to do that the Israelites refused to follow his lead and attacked the Canaanites in an attempt to take back the land they lives in before they moved to Egypt. It was these actions that created a darker reality and unhealthy collective spirit of mankind. The third scene of the prophecy includes seven angels filled with plagues holding cups. The collective spirit of mankind is filled with plagues because of the actions described in the Bible's stories of Exodus and the Old Testament. It is not that the Israelites created all the unhealthiness of our collective spirit but that mankind lived this way and we all created the unhealthy nature of our collective spirit.

This 6th angel with a trumpet measures the kingdom of the heavens to determine what level of emotional content and higher consciousness exists in the collective spirit of mankind. It is found that little to no spiritual growth existed and this is why Jesus came to help. It was the results of his efforts to live with a loving and forgiving spirit that made the difference. He planted these seeds of forgiveness and love in the collective spirit of mankind and we have become the fruits of his labor as we have now learned to grow our spirits into a better light. We have expanded our presence in the kingdom of the heavens as we now exist with spirits that are both learning to love and not learning to love. It is the attempts to forgive and love that have allowed us to grow into this better light and for future generations to use this better light to make the world a better place.

The dragon and two beasts represent a lifetime filled with change and spiritual growth that ends with a new reality being created generation after generation and lifetime after lifetime. This is the end result of mankind's evolution into a world that recognizes that we are all one and that we do create collectively, together. In the first two times of mankind's existence we only knew about the impact of our tribes and then the nations that we were a part of. Now over the last 2,000 years we have completed the evolution that began with the expansion of the Roman Empire and China. We have now grown into One World, United (and still uniting) as one as we have finally realized that we all effect and impact one another.

THE DRAGON AND TWO BEASTS SUMMARIZED

There is a strategy used to make these changes a reality in our lives. There is a mission or greater purpose for this 75 year life cycle that comes from our prayers and deep rooted desires to make this world a better place. When anyone reaches deep into their heart and soul with a desire to make the world a better place their prayers are heard. A deep rooted feeling and the desire that accompanies it crates the spirit of the prayer. The spirit of these prayers becomes the spirit of the purpose or mission of future generations of children. A generation of children will enter the world with the spirit necessary to complete this purpose. Their greater spirit comes with a higher consciousness needed to complete the changes prayed for by those that lived in the previous live time.

The strategy used by creation to transform the collective spirit of mankind has three parts to it:

1) To use the first generation to bring a new spirit in to the way of life that exists in the world.
2) To use the second generation to allow a new consciousness into the reality of this change.
3) To use the third generation to bring about a new reality in the physical world (collective body), the collective spirit, collective consciousness (collective soul) and the ambient spirit that exists in the air around us.

Every lifetime is about 75 years long, Therefore about every 22 years a new generation releases its spirit into the world.

THE GREAT WINEPRESS (THE LAST HALF OF THE 3 ½ GENERATIONS THAT EXIST IN A LIFE TIME)

A wine press transforms individual grapes into the collective fluid of wine. In the same way the prophecy refers to this process of transformation as a person's spirit is transformed from one reality into another. As a person takes his journey from light to dark this wine press will feel like the wrath of God has been unleashed on him or her; when on his or her quest to create a light based spirit this transformation allows a person to feel God's compassion. The prophecy was talking about how the spirit of the Israelites felt the wrath of God 2,000 years ago as their spirit was broken many years before the days Jesus walked the earth.

As our lives are ending and a generation of people have lived their life and accomplished their purpose(s) they will leave this world a better place than it was when they came into it. As they leave they are transformed into the afterlife AND when they return in a future lifetime they will be transformed into their higher vibrating reality as this process of re-creation continues to make this world a better place.

This wine press transforms all creations that evolve from dark to light of from light to dark. At the time of the prophecy the transformations that existed were going into darker realities so phrases like the wrath of God were appropriate. Today the transformation could be more about receiving the compassion of God. It is about an individual person's spirit evolving into a bright light reality of the greater light of the collective consciousness. It is also about the integration of the ambient spirit of mankind's creations that will be integrated into a state oneness when the spirit of Babylon becomes one with the light based collective spirit of mankind.

The last reality that this image represents is the process of incarnation (or reincarnation).

INCARNATION/REINCARNATION – THE CONTINUITY OF MY PERSONAL SPIRIT OR THE CONTINUITY OF THE COLLECTIVE SPIRIT OF MANKIND

When you put all the pieces of the puzzle of life together, you get a different understanding of reincarnation. Think about it this way. You lived a life thousands of years ago when the way of life in the world was filled with much harsher realities than today. During that life time your spirit was broken into say five pieces.

Q: When you die; what happens to those five pieces?

A: they continue to exist independently as five lives.

When you die they just continue on in their own existence. In future lives they would be considered your soul mates. As time goes on they continue to have lives filled with hardships and then continue to breakdown into smaller pieces. Then at a point in time in the recreation of the collective spirit of mankind we begin to evolve thru this healing process and our spirits are no longer breaking down but instead recreating its-self. When the collective journey became a quest we began to recreate our spirit and soul as we healed these broken parts of our spirits. Throughout a lifetime, several of these parts of these broken spirits evolve into a higher light and are harvested into the light side of the kingdom of the heavens. When these separate spirits are ready to re-enter the world and have another life they can reunite in one body and have a life that will allow them to learn how to live together as one body, spirit and soul again. In this way they are the greater light of a generation of children that will enter the world to continue this process of re-creation.

The challenge to the concept of reincarnation is that we never return as the same person we were in the past life. We are either entering the world as a smaller spirit when we were on our journey into a darker reality or we enter as a greater spirit and higher consciousness when we are on our quest to recreate a spirit that was broken many lifetimes ago. If reincarnation is defined as the continuity of the life of my personal spirit; it is hard to say that when I reunite with other parts of what used to be me that I am still the same spirit that existed in a past life. I am obviously not the same spirit or person I was when I died in a past life; therefore there is no continuity of life that could possibly exist.

Perhaps the continuity of life relates more to the collective spirit of mankind and that which we create collectively through our thoughts, words and actions.

The seven angels with plagues holding seven cups explain how we created the spirit of Babylon and it kings. As you read about the great city of Babylon you learn that there are kings that rule our lives. These kings are the forces created by the collective spirit in each of the seven churches. The power they had on our lives (and still have on many people) was (is) overwhelming. It was during the era of the spirit of Babylon that mankind found its prodigal son moment and collectively we began our quest to find our light again. It was when we accepted that we can destroy ourselves that we became committed to this process of re-creating our spirit.

These seven angels with seven trumpets represent the collective spirit of the Israelites and mankind after we existed for about 1,700 years without the ability to transform our spirits from dark to light. They tell the story of how we created Babylon and they explain how the process of living with love (overcoming the darker realities of our creations) works. The best way to explain this is read the seven angels with seven trumpets simultaneously with these seven angels with cups. As you read the prophecies quotes about the first cup, you will also read the quote from the first trumpet. This way you can see how these two images are linked both in the creation of Babylon and its history as well as how the process of forgiving and living with love work together. Each of the first four trumpets will be presented in the same way. Because the length of the explanation for the fifth, sixth and seventh trumpets and cups can be rather lengthy, only the dialogue about these last three cups will be presented.

The prophecies introduction to this part of the scene is listed below:

> *"And I saw another sign in heaven, great and wonderful: seven angels that had seven plagues which are the last; for by them the wrath of God is brought to an end*
>
> *And I saw, as it were, a sea of glass mingled with fire, and those who had obtained the victory over the beast, and over his image, and over the number of his name, standing on the sea of glass, having the harps of God. And they sung the song of Moses the servant of God, and the song of the Lamb, saying: Great and wonderful are thy works, Lord God Almighty; just and true are thy ways, thou King of saints. Who will not fear thee, O Lord, and glorify thy name? For thou alone art holy; for all nations shall come and worship before thee, because thy judgments are made manifest."* (REV. 15:1 – 15:4)

This is where the prophecy begins talking about people that have deal with their issues in life and begin their quest to find their light again. They are on their path to leave the grasp of the collective spirit of mankind had on them when it was filled with plagues. To repent is to forgive those that hurt you and then to leave the way of life that existed when you were one with the darker realities of the collective spirit of mankind. This is what the prophecy is referring to when it says *"… those who had obtained the victory over the beast, and over his image and over the number of his name…"*

And after this I saw, and the temple of the tabernacle of the testimony in heaven was opened; and the seven angels that had the seven plagues came out of the temple, clothed in pure white linen, and girded about the breasts with golden girdles. And one of the four living creatures gave to the seven angels seven golden cups full of the wrath of God, who lives from age to age. And the temple was filled with smoke from the glory of God, and from his power; and no one was able to enter the temple, till the seven plagues of the seven angels were completed." (REV. 15:5 – 15:8)

In the previous scene with seven angels with seven trumpets there were angels that sounded there trumpets and plagues were released into mankind's collective spirit. The next scene has seven angels filled with plagues and holding seven cups. The big picture reality of these seven angels with seven cups is about learning to live your life in such a way as to maintain your light. The seven trumpets are about learning to forgive; this raises your spirits vibration making it strong enough to hold light. Then these seven cups fill your spirit with the light needed so you can feel love. This scene is about the next evolution of our collective spirits. It is about three realities:

1) That which we will create while our spirits are filled with these plagues. We created what the prophecy refers as Babylon. Babylon is the purposeful nature of what was created as a result of the Roman Empires strategy to conquer, suppress and control those within the empire.
2) How this part of the healing process will work to transform our spirits from dark to light. The trumpets were about evolving through the lesser light of the heavens and these cups explain the process of evolving through the greater light of the heavens.
3) They explain how our spirits work when they are filled with passion. Whether that passion comes from a positive or negative reality does not matter. Living with our spirits filled with passion is just another reality of creation.

Until this scene there was only creation of the individual person's body, spirit and soul and the collective spirit of mankind. Now we add another reality of creation – The ambient spirit of that which we create through our thoughts, words and actions. The ambient spirit is referred to as Babylon.

At the time of the prophecy mankind's collective spirit was filled with wrath. When the prophecy says that an angel is going to pour out a cup of God's wrath, it is referring to the collective spirit of mankind being filled with wrath and what we created with it.

Much like the first four angels with trumpets these angels with angels with cups pour there cups into the earth, seas, rivers and streams and the sun, moon and stars. The prophecy tells the story of the evolution of the collective spirit of mankind. This story began with seven churches with an angel in each church, the first evolution was the seven seal and then the seven angels with seven trumpets and now the final evolution of the prophecy is illustrated as seven angels with seven cups. To best tell this story we have to link all of these together. This will explain the matrix of the prophecy.

"And I heard a great voice out of the temple, saying to the seven angels: Go and pour out the seven cups of the wrath of God upon the earth." (REV. 16:1)

As mankind grew into the darkest reality of our creations we learned to survive with a constant flow of wrath. As these angels pour their cups of the wrath of God they are filling the seven parts of our spirits with wrath as if our spirits were cups waiting to be filled. When our spirits are weak and not capable of holding light they will be filled with the wrath of God. When our spirits are strong enough to hold light they will be filled with compassion and more than just love. When strong enough to hold light there are many realities in which we use love to create things like acceptance, mercy, peace, faith and more.

The prophecies' introductory statement about these cups said that there were people that had obtained victory over the beast; those that did not achieve this victory still had the mark of the beast and worshipped his image. When people live with a spirit that is filled with plagues they are only capable of living with the suffering that comes with a spirit not capable of holding light. When mankind is filled with a darker reality and continues to feed off of it we create more of the anger, hatred, wrath etc. that we are consumed with. This is what this cup is referring to. When this first part of the collective spirit of mankind pours its cup into a person's spirit; it impacts those that have not grown beyond the darker reality of the collective spirit of mankind.

The First Angel Sounding a Trumpet

"And the first sounded; and there was hail and fire mingled with blood, and it was thrown into the earth; and the third part of the earth was burned up, and the third part of the trees was burned up, and all green grass was burned up." (REV. 8:7)

The First Angel Filled with Plagues Holding a Cup

"And the first angel went, and poured out his cup on the land; and there came a hurtful and afflictive sore upon the men that had the mark of the beast, and that worshiped his image." (REV. 16:2)

The first angels with a trumpet and a cup relate to the fire that came from the Israelites as they walked in the desert for 40 years. The fire that was created because the relationships that should have existed between them and God, Nature and Creation left them and was replaced with the rage that existed in their spirits was sent into the earth.

As they continued to live in this state unhappiness the spirit of their rage and the gluttonous nature of creation continued to feed them more of the rage they felt for thousands of years grew into the destructive nature of the first angel with a plague holding a cup.

As the Israelites lived with the rage that existed in their spirits nature continued to take it and hold it for them. At this point in evolution the Israelites were not the only ones that lived this way. The relationships that should have existed between them and the rest of the peoples of the Middle East is what was broken. As this relationship continued to be destroyed there was even more destruction that mankind created.

I hope you can see how the breakdown in relationships destroys all of us. This is the primary message of the prophecy. In this first angel with trumpet and a cup it is the breakdown in the relationship between a person and all of mankind, mankind and nature and finally between man and creation. Only by rebuilding these relationships will we release the seal that sealed our fate. It is the message of the seven churches of the first scene that tell us how to release these seals – forgive and live with love. Then the destructive nature of mankind kind will begin to transform into a creation based reality.

This first cup says that by overcoming the forces that make us feel as if the hurtful things we do are acceptable will we no longer worship the beast (human nature that comes from the collective spirit of mankind) will be able to no longer feel the pain and suffering that so many people live within their day to day lives.

The Second Angel Sounding a Trumpet

"And the second angel sounded; and as it were a great mountain burning with fire was cast into the sea; and the third part of the sea became blood, and the third part of the creatures that were in the sea, that had life, died, and the third part of the ships were destroyed." (REV. 8:8 – 8:9)

The Second Angel Filled with Plagues Holding a Cup

"And the second angel poured out his cup on the sea; and it became blood, like that of a dead man; and every soul in the sea died." (REV. 16:3)

The second part of your spirit is about a lack of love of self and the lust that replaces it. Hatred is the primary emotions that a person creates through when their spirit is filled with lust. To replace lust with love of self will transform the destructive nature of the blood that made every soul in the sea die with the blood of life.

Love of self is a powerful force in creation. It occurs when a person's spirit attracts its body, spirit and soul toward one another. Without love of self these components of creation repel one another away from each other. I hope you can now see the importance of transforming this repelling force into an attracting force so we can then find our love of self. When a person transforms his spirit in to this reality of creation others will sense and feel the love of self and confidence that comes with it when they meet this person. This reality will then create a natural feeling of being attracted to this person that has the power of love of self, flowing through his or her spirit. When mankind has evolved into this reality of love of self we will be ready to create healthier relationships with one another and collectively the world will be ready to forgive itself.

In a similar way to the first angel, this second angel represents the hatred that people feel for each other and how nature takes it from us and holds it for us until we can deal with it in a future lifetime. We are all connected to nature and nature is connected to us. One way to think of it is like this, "What we create nature becomes". The first angel represents how the earth is connected to this first part of our spirit. This second angel is about the spirit of the seas and oceans being connected to the second part of our spirit. The third angel and fourth angel are connected to the rivers and streams and sun, moon and stars, respectively. This is the matrix of creation. The seven parts of our spirit and the seven parts of the spirit of all of nature are one in nature. We are nature and nature is us. When our spirit is filled with plagues (unhealthy) the spirit of all of nature is a reflection of us. When we live with fear and express anger, hatred and rage we fill nature with what we are at that moment in time. Nature then becomes one with us and as we deal with the issues in our lives that caused the fear, anger etc.... we cleanse not only our spirit but the spirit of nature also. This is why it takes generations of children living many lifetimes to fix what was broken so many thousands of years ago.

When the prophecy says, "the second angel poured out his cup on the sea" it simply means the hatred that existed in the second part of our broken spirit was filled with hatred and the seas naturally took this from us. The seas became blood like that of a dead man. Then the hatred killed every soul in the sea. The souls of those that were positive became negative. This means that fish and all animals that lived in the sea went from a positive spirit to a negative spirit and their souls were dead to creation. As mankind learns to love again these seas will no longer flow with the blood of a dead man, we will replace it with the blood of life. This will transform the relationships that animals have with each other and with mankind into a much more positive and creation based relationship. This is seen in many ways as people and animals are rebuilding their relationships and creating love based friendships with one another. The antagonistic nature of man and beasts is changing and will continue to evolve as we evolve. We are the leaders of this pack and have to create the kind of relationships we want to exist with.

This is the reality that occurs in nature when someone loses their love of self. When we love our self we are more capable of loving others. These are the foundations of love that are necessary to create before we can truly and deeply love family and close friends.

The Third Angel Sounding a Trumpet

And the third angel sounded; and there fell from heaven a great star burning as a lamp, and it fell upon the third part of the rivers and upon the fountains of waters. And the name of the star is called Wormwood. And the third part of the waters became wormwood, and many men died of the waters, because they were made bitter. (Rev.8:10 – 8:11)

The Third Angel Filled with Plagues Holding a Cup

"And the third angel poured out his cup on the rivers and the fountains of waters; and they became blood. And I heard the angel of the waters, saying: Just art thou, who art and who wast, the Holy One, because thou hast thus judged. For they have shed the blood of saints and of prophets, and thou hast given them blood to drink, and they are worthy. And

I heard a voice from the altar saying: Even so, Lord God Almighty, true and just are thy judgments." (REV. 16:4 – 16:7)

This third angel is about love of family, greed and fear based anger. As the Israelites lived alone in the desert dishonored by the Egyptians, disrespected by the others in the Middle East and lived a disheartening life in the desert their spirits were more than broken. This led to the bitterness they felt towards mankind in general. They had to survive and did what they had to do to survive. Many are still very unforgiving of them. Interesting how those that could have offered them a hand, could have brought them into their lives and helped them but instead lived to punish them still continue to feed off what was created almost 4,000 years ago. They did exactly what anyone else in that time period would have done if they were in the same situation. As a matter of fact most people in that time period probably would not have waited 40 years to attack another nation and survive.

The bitterness of the feelings between the Israelites and others in the Middle East is what is represented by this third angel. The last phrase of the angel with a trumpet says, *"because they were made bitter"*. It was not just the bitterness of the Israelites but also the bitterness of the Egyptians and so many others that caused this reality in nature.

The judgment referred to in this statement from the angel with a cup is about how creation judged them by allowing the darkness of their creation to become complete. When we are at the depth of our darkest moments is when we will find our first light and then have the opportunity to create our brightest light.

This statement has two meanings one is that mankind collectively grew into this darkest time in the evolution of our spirits and souls. This is when we had our prodigal son moment and began to transform our spirits into a better light. Our quest began somewhere in the past 2,000 years. The other part of this statement will come when mankind rekindles its love for one another completely. It is when Islam and Israel heal from the wounds of the past. When they can deeply and sincerely forgive one another for the sins of their past the healing of this part of the collective spirit begins. When mankind as a whole, follows their lead and deals with their issues in life and learn to forgive and live with love in a New World with Order and Peace that this statement comes to fruition.

Fourth Angel Sounding a Trumpet

"And the fourth angel sounded; and the third part of the sun was smitten, and the third part of the moon, and the third part of the stars, that the third part of them might be darkened, and the day might not shine for the third part of it, and the night likewise. And I saw, and heard an eagle flying in the midst of heaven, saying with a loud voice: Woe, woe, woe to them that dwell on the earth because of the rest of the voices of the trumpet of the three angels that are about to sound." (REV. 8:12 – 8:13)

The Fourth Angel Filled with Plagues Holding a Cup

> *"And the fourth angel poured out his cup on the sun; and it was given to him to scorch men with fire. And men were scorched with great heat; and they uttered impious words against the name of God who has power over these plagues; and they repented not, that they might give him glory."* (REV. 16:8 – 16:9)

Fear is the primary feeling that this fourth angel is all about. Fear in a spiritually healthy human being is a powerful tool to use in our lives. Fear can tell us when danger exists in our lives and then we will be guided to avoid dangerous situations. When a person or groups of people are in an environment that is dangerous our spirits fill with fear. When there is nothing we can do to avoid the danger our spirit will fill with fear and/or terror and we will feel afraid. To be filled with fear for a prolonged period of time is to be fearful. This leads to creating the first seal that seals our fate into a darker reality.

Fear is stored in the heavens; in the sun, moon and stars. Fear is the underlying emotion for all that is created from greed, lust, gluttony, sloth, pride and envy. It is the vastness of the heavens that is needed to hold all the fear that comes from this lack of compassion (love of those that wish us harm). When mankind is ready to live without fear we will be ready to create a world filled with peace.

Fifth Angel Sounding a Trumpet

> *"And the fifth angel sounded: and I saw a star that had fallen from heaven to the earth, and to him was given the key of the pit of the abyss. And he opened the pit of the abyss; and there arose out of the pit a smoke as the smoke of a great furnace, and the sun and the air were darkened by means of the smoke of the pit. And out of the smoke came forth locusts upon the earth, and to them was given power as the scorpions of the earth have power. And it was said to them that they should not hurt the grass of the earth, neither any green thing nor any tree, but the men such as have not the seal of God in their foreheads. And it was given to them that they should not kill them, but that they should be tormented five months; and this torment is as the torment of a scorpion, when he strikes a man. And in those days men shall seek death and shall not find it, and they shall desire to die and death flees from them. … The first woe has past: behold, there come two woes more after this."* (Rev. 9:1 – 9:12)

The first four angels with trumpets were about creating seals that sealed mankind's spirit into a darker reality. They also explained how the spirit of nature absorbed the darker feelings, emotions and memories (creations) of the Israelites and mankind. When these seals were released it was only natural that mankind would have to evolve into a darker reality before we would be able to begin our quest to create light. This fifth trumpet sounded as mankind dis-evolved into the abyss. The collective spirit of mankind was on its journey; as we lived with the reality of the first four seals it was only natural that we would slip into the abyss of the heavens. This is why the prophecy says that these scorpions were not to harm nature but the men that have not received the seal of God. Mankind would have to live with a collective spirit that was in the darkest realities of life before we would be able to find our way out of the darkness that we created.

The Fifth Angel Filled with Plagues Holding a Cup

"And the fifth angel poured out his cup on the throne of the beast; and his kingdom was filled with darkness; and they gnawed their tongues because of pain; and they spoke impiously against the God of heaven because of their pains, and because of their sores; and they repented not of their works." (REV. 16:10- 16:11)

Throughout this book I have mentioned that we all have our prodigal son moment and when we do we learn to deal with our issues in life (repent/forgive). Without this prodigal son moment we will just remain in a state of mind that perpetuates the darker realities of living a life sealed away from love and light. This angel pours its cup on the throne of the beast in two ways:

1) As the darker spirit of our past sins continue to enter our lives lifetime after lifetime eventually we will reach that point when we accept that we are sleeping with the pigs. We will then begin the process of repent and overcome.

2) When people have learned to deal with their issues in life we will naturally stop worshipping the beast as we leave the darker reality of the collective spirit that wants to perpetuate itself. As we create a reality in the collective spirit of mankind where we have a bright light in our spirit, this light will shine brightly within everyone. This light shining within everyone will make those that still worship the beast feel even more uncomfortable doing so. This will naturally motivate them to deal with their issues because this light will help to create their prodigal son moment.

It is important to note a similarity between the sixth angel with a trumpet and the angel with the fifth cup. These two parts of the prophecy are saying that we do get better over time.

The sixth angel sounds a trumpet

"And the rest of men, that were not killed by these plagues, repented not of the works of their hands, that they should not worship demons and idols of gold and of silver and of brass and of stone and of wood, which can neither see, nor hear, nor walk, and they repented not of their murders, neither of their sorceries nor of their lewdness nor of their thefts." (REV. 9:20 – 9:21)

FIFTH CUP

"... they repented not of their works." (REV. 16:11)

The importance of these statements is that between the time of the angel with sixth trumpet and the angel with the fifth cup people have learned to repent from

1) That they should not worship demons and idols of gold and of silver and of brass and of stone and of wood, which can neither see, nor hear, nor walk.
2) They repented not of their murders, neither of their sorceries nor of their lewdness nor of their thefts.

What it is saying is that people do learn from the book of knowledge that their thoughts, words and actions do matter. We all learn that worshipping people and our relationships with nature our- self and one another are the only things that matter. We will also learn the difference between manifestation and creation and learn to create. It is only natural to grow into this state reality. It is not to say that those that practice manifestation today are doing something wrong. It is just saying that when we get to the point in our spiritual evolution and realize that we no longer need to manifest in order to feel comfortable in our lives we will have grown spiritually.

Then we will learn to deal with our past life issues. Through dealing with past life issues and forgiving the sins of the past we will evolve into the brightest light possible. This is when people learn to forgive groups of people and organizations like the Roman Empire, the Catholic Church, Islam and Israel and many others for their sins of the past.

An example is:

Today many people hold resentment towards the Catholic Church because of things the Church did 500 or 1,000 years ago. They feel as if they should hold the church accountable and even punish the church for events that occurred in the past. The reason we are feeling this anger, rage and resentment is because it is time to learn to forgive and love, not to perpetuate the darkness of the sins of the past.

The Sixth Angel Filled with Plagues Holding a Cup

"And the sixth angel poured out his cup on the great river Euphrates; and its water was dried up, that the way of the kings of the east might be prepared. And I saw three unclean spirits, like frogs, come out of the mouth of the dragon, and out of the mouth of the beast; and out of the mouth of the false prophet. For they are the spirits of demons that do signs, and they go forth to the kings of the whole world, to bring them together to the battle of that great day of God Almighty. Behold, I come as a thief: blessed is he that watches, and keeps his garments, that he may not walk naked, and that men may not see his nakedness. And they brought them together into a place that is called, in the Hebrew tongue, Armageddon". (REV. 16:12 – 16:16)

This statement simply means that a person has dealt with the sins of his or her past all the way back to the beginning of time. The beginning of time relates to the days of Adam and Eve and the first reality of the broken spirit which was Adam. In the beginning there was the Garden of Eden and four rivers that flowed from it. The fourth river was Euphrates. When we have collectively dealt with all the issues in our lives that created the darkness that plagued our spirits and soul for thousands of years we will have reached this point in the collective healing of mankind. The darker realities of the spirit of mankind will leave the collective spirit of mankind (human nature will change permanently) is what is symbolized as three frog like spirits that leave the dragon, the beast and the false prophet.

One way to explain this reality of the healing process is best explained by using one of the Greek gods Narcissus.

> Pride filled this god. Pride was so powerful within him that he adored himself more than others. What should have been love for others became distain for them. There just is not enough room in ones heart for love of others when you love yourself in this way. Nemesis (another Greek god) noticed his need to love himself and his physical looks. Nemesis attracted Narcissus to a pool, where he saw his own reflection in the water and fell in love with it, not realizing it was merely an image. He was so fixated on his own image that he could not leave his reflection. He no longer had a desire to live and stayed there staring at his reflection until he died.

When mankind learns to overcome the prideful, narcissistic nature of the spirit of narcissism we will reject the spirit of it from within us. As the spirit of it leaves the collective spirit of mankind it will be the beginning of the transformation of this ancient god. At this point the transformation is not complete. The spirit of these frogs still exists in the ambient air around us. When se live with this reality in our lives for thousands of years we create it in the air around us and we still have to deal with this reality of creation. In the future we will have to resist the temptation to allow it to return to our personal spirit(s). By not feeding it we will allow it to get smaller and smaller until it disintegrates and will no longer be a part of our individual and collective reality.

Those that maintain the light of their spirits will create a new ambient spirit. As you will read in the next few chapters this is when we are able to transform the darker spirit called "Babylon" into what the prophecy refers to as "The New Holy City of Jerusalem". This is why it is important to keep your garments clean by maintaining your light.

The Seventh Angel Filled with Plagues Holding a Cup

> *"And the seventh angel poured out his cup into the air; and there came a great voice from the temple of heaven, from the throne, saying: It is done."* (REV. 16:17)

This simply means that the end of a time in creation has occurred. This end of time is when mankind has created the collective spirit in such a way as to have people that live with spirits that are dark, light and bright. When some people live with anger and are still sealed into a darker reality while others are learning to create a light spirit and others live with a bright spirit the collective spirit of mankind will exist in all three parts of the heavens. When people live together with this full range of emotions it will be very difficult for everyone to see eye to eye and to get along with one another. For example, people that need to live with pride while others have no wants or needs will have a unique set of challenges to deal with as they try to get along with one another. The next time will be when all of mankind evolves into the bright light of the heavens and we are then capable of creating an ambient spirit that is a reflection of the collective spirit of mankind when we are all living in the bright light of the heavens.

THE PROPHECIES MESSAGE TO MANKIND FOR THIS SCENE

Everything we say think and do collectively creates a very powerful reality in creation. This ambient spirit of mankind that today is about business systems used to be what many referred to as the gods of their nation or tribe. The power of creation is not about my personal power to create but more importantly our power to create collectively.

This power to create; that we have, always has been and always will be transformative in nature.

The power of children and generations of children entering the world with a collective spirit can and will transform the collective spirit of mankind and the ambient spirit of the world. These generations will change the reality of our lives. The more we help the younger generation make this world a better place the better off we will all be in the long run. This will then replace the destructive nature of the third part of man into a creation based reality.

THE MYSTERY OF BABYLON - BABYLON IS THE HARLOT THAT RIDES THE BEAST

This is the first time the prophecy refers to the spirit of that which we create (the ambient spirit of mankind). The prophecy shows a woman with a cup filled with the impurities of the world. The cup represents the intention and purpose filled nature of mankind when we created and perpetuated this gluttonous lust filled spirit. Her name is Babylon and she is referred to as the Great City that is now divided. She rides the beast and is consumed by her own lustful nature.

In this part of the third scene is another riddle. It is the mystery of the great Harlot. The following is an explanation of this riddle. The riddle explains the Harlot and the beast as the collective spirit of mankind and how we created the spirit of Babylon. It describes the beast as having seven heads and ten horns which is the collective spirit of mankind when we are learning to cleanse our spirits of the sins of the past. It describes the seven heads and ten horns of the beast as kings and mountains. It describes seven mountains with a king for each mountain. The mountains are the mountains of issues that rule our lives when we are in a darker reality in our collective existence. When we have all these issues in our lives they rule our lives. It is like they have a life of their own and control us. The collective spirit of each of these mountains is the kings that rule our lives. As the collective spirit of mankind evolves into a bright light three more kings will exist as we learn to deal with more of the issues that await us.

This image is about mankind's collective spirit (the beast) creating the spirit of Babylon (the ambient spirit of mankind). Earlier the prophecy talks about four riders on horses; they symbolized how we ride these horses wildly into the darkness of our realities. This symbolized how we created the collective spirit of mankind. Now the prophecy is showing us how the collective spirit of mankind creates the ambient spirit that is in the air around us.

When the prophecy was shown to St. John this is how it represented mankind creating and living with the spirit of that which we will need to re-create. The prophecy refers to Babylon as the great city that is divided into three parts. These three parts have to be viewed from two perspectives 1) the individual spirit, collective spirit and the ambient spirit that exists when; 2) the kingdom of the heavens has evolved to include people that exist in the dark, light and bright of the heavens.

It is divided into three parts when we evolve into a reality that is the dark, light and bright of the kingdom of the heavens. When we collectively evolve and the collective spirit of mankind expands in such a way as to contain people that are in the darker regions, lighter regions and brighter regions of the heavens we will have divided the collective spirit of mankind into three cities. When mankind reaches this level of evolution we will create a reality and way of life that exists with all three creating the ambient spirit that we need in order to survive, live and thrive. This will then create a new reality where people will live with spirits that are filled with wrath, learning to live with love and live with love. The prophecy goes from explaining how this city of Babylon will be transformed into the New Holy City of Jerusalem.

Then as we continue our evolution into a collective spirit that is only a bright light we will begin to create the New Holy City of Jerusalem. This fully integrated society will be healthy, wealthy and wise. As you will read in the next chapter of this book this fully integrated collective body, spirit and soul will have 12 foundations and 4 walls with 3 gates on each wall and these walls will be 12,000 cubits high and 12,000 cubits wide and 144,000 furlongs long. The foundations are built on the creation of love, mercy, acceptance, peace, wisdom, faith and more. This New Holy City occurs as we transform collectively into a greater light and then transition into a greater spiritual reality and finally transcend into an angelic reality as we become the angel we are supposed to be.

This prophecy is about the re-creation of the broken spirit of an angel and this final stage in our evolution is when we become one again in pure consciousness.

CHAPTER 5

THE NEW HOLY CITY OF JERUSALEM

TRANSFORMING YOUR BODY, SPIRIT AND SOUL INTO A HIGHER LIGHT AND THE TRANSFORMATION OF BABYLON INTO THE NEW HOLY CITY OF JERUSALEM

Babylon is Divided into Three Parts & The Fall of Babylon

The Marriage Supper of the Lamb

The Devil is Chained for 1,000 Years and then Released

The Marriage of the Lamb and the Bride - The New Holy City of Jerusalem

The New Holy City of Jerusalem

    1) its foundations:
        a) there are 12 foundations
        b) each foundation has the name of the 12 Apostles written on them
        c) each foundation is adorned in 1 of 12 crystals
    2) its walls:
        a) there are 4 walls each having 3 gates
        b) these walls are 12,000 cubits wide and 12,000 cubits high
        c) the city is 144,000 cubits long

THE INTEGRATION OF THE SPIRIT AND SOUL AND THE CREATION OF THE AMBIENT SPIRIT OF MANKIND IS DESCRIBED IN THIS LAST SCENE OF THE PROPHECY.

AS YOU NOW KNOW THE FIRST SCENE WAS ABOUT THE SON OF MAN (THE BROKEN SOUL) AND SEVEN CHURCHES (THE BROKEN SPIRIT).

THEN MANKIND HAD TO LEARN TO TRANSFORM ITS SPIRIT AND SOUL INTO A LIGHT BASED REALITY. BUT IT DID NOT WORK. JESUS CAME TO FIX THE PROBLEM BUT THERE WAS ANOTHER COMPONENT IN CREATION THAT EXISTED – BABYLON.

AT THIS POINT IN TIME THERE WAS INDIVIDUAL PEOPLE AND THEIR SPIRITS, THE COLELCTIVE SPIRIT OF MANKIND AND THE AMBIENT SPIRIT OF OUR CREATIONS. ALL THREE HAVE TO BE INTEGRATED INTO ONE BEFORE OUR JOB IS DONE.

THIS FINAL SCENE OF THE PROPHECY EXPLAINS HOW THIS WILL HAPPEN.

<u>RELEASING THE SEALS THAT SEALED THE BOOK OF KNOWLEDGE OF LOVE AND LIGHT THAT SEALED OUR FATE.</u>

<u>THE TRANSFORMATION INTO AN EMOTIONAL REALITY</u> - THE SPIRIT AND SOUL LEARNS TO LIVE WITH GREATER EMOTIONS AND A HIGHER CONSCIOUSNESS.

THEN THE <u>TRANSITION INTO A SPIRITUAL BEING</u> WILL OCCUR AS THE SPIRIT AND SOUL BECOME ONE BEING OF LOVE AND LIGHT AGAIN.

THE FALL OF BABYLON OCCURS WHEN WE NO LONGER CREATE THROUGH THE LOWER ANGER BASED REALITIES. AS WE LEARN TO JUST BE AND ALLOW CREATION TO EXIST AS IT SHOULD BE WE WILL NO LONGER FEED THE SPIRIT OF BABYLON OR BE FED BY IT. WE WILL ALSO NATURALLY ALLOW CREATION TO JUST "BE" THROUGHOUT OUR EXISTENCE AS THE NEW HOLY CITY OF JERUSALEM BECOMES ONE WITH OUR NEW REALITY.

A SENSE OF ONENESS IN BODY, SPIRIT AND SOUL WILL CREATE A REALITY THAT SEPARATES OUR SPIRIT FROM THE DARKER FORCES THAT EXIST IN THE KINGDOM OF THE HEAVENS. THERE IS STILL WORK TO BE DONE AND THIS SEPARATION GIVES PEOPLE THE OPPORTUNITY TO LEARN TO LIVE IN THIS NEW REALITY.

THEN THERE IS A TIME WHEN YOU (WE) WILL BE TESTED TO SEE IF WE CAN MAINTAIN YOUR LIGHT WHEN TEMPTED BY THESE DARKER FORCES AGAIN.

WHEN YOU (WE) HAVE PASSED THESE TESTS WE ARE READY FOR OUR <u>TRANSCENDANCE BEYOND THE KINGDOM OF THE HEAVENS AS AN ANGELIC BEING</u> INTO THE KINGDOM OF GOD – THE PURE CONSCIOUSNESS OF THE NEW HOLY CITY OF JERUSALEM.

THEN THE MARRIAGE OF THE LAMB AND THE BRIDE COMPLETES THE INTEGRATION OF THAT WHICH WE CREATE AS ONE. TO BE ONE WITH OUR CREATION IN THIS FINAL DESTINATION IS TO EXIST IN AN ANGELIC SPIRITUAL REALITY AND BE WHO WE ARE AND CREATE WHAT WE ARE.

Babylon is the end result of mankind's collective creations over the 1,700 years after Moses left the Israelites until the time of Jesus. It is the gluttonous, lustful reality that exists because the Israelites and mankind lived with a collective spirit that was not strong enough to hold light. The prophecy describes Babylon after the seven angels with plagues pour their cups into nature and throughout the world. These cups represent how mankind lived with a sense of purpose when our spirits were weak. When our spirits were weak our soul and its consciousness was not able to guide us in such a way as to create anything except the destructive reality that existed then and is still present in the world today. In the prophecy cups represent living with purpose. It is how we fil our spirits the passion. We fill our spirits with the emotion and consciousness that is a reflection of who we are (the light or dark of the collective spirit of mankind). The seven parts of the spirit of mankind were seen as being filled with plagues. Filled with plagues means the collective spirit was not pure. When mankind was consumed by this lower vibrating purpose we created hell on earth.

The seven angels with seven cups are also about the repent and overcome healing process. The "forgive and live with love" process is illustrated through the seven angels with seven trumpets (forgive) and seven cups (live with love). The images and symbols of the prophecy are about mankind's journey into darkness and our quest to create a light based collective spirit. When the seven cups are poured out and our collective spirit is no longer filled with plagues, mankind will have learned to live with love. This is when Babylon begins to be divided into three parts. The collective spirit of mankind will have a bright light component, a light component and a dark component when Babylon is divided into three parts. When we create through these three components Babylon will be divided into three parts because Babylon (the collective spirit of mankind) will be a reflection of who we are. We will exist with these three parts until the darker and light components evolve into the bright light of the heavens.

The spirit of Babylon is what we created when the collective spirit of mankind was in a very dark reality. Basically, there are three realities that mankind will evolve into – A dark reality, a reality in which we are learning to live with a light based spirit and a reality in which we are living with a spirit capable of holding a bright light. When the spirit of Babylon began mankind was sealed in a darker reality. We are currently beginning to create the reality in which we are learning about love; therefore the collective spirit of mankind exists in both the dark and the light. In the future the collective spirit of mankind will exist simultaneously, in all three realities. When this reality of evolution comes to fruition we will create the ambient spirit all three realities. We will have to learn to live together in this reality. This is when Babylon will be divided into three parts. The final evolution is when the collective spirit of mankind exists only in the bright light of the heavens. This reality is referred to as the fall of Babylon. Without being motivated by the wants and needs, desires and cravings of a lower vibrating reality we will no longer create through the same forces that created Babylon and we will no longer feed of feed off of the spirit of Babylon. This is what the fall of Babylon is all about.

Here we will collectively create a different spirit of Babylon and a peaceful reality in our lives. This is what the prophecy refers to as, "The Fall of Babylon".

AN EXAMPLE OF WHAT WE CREATED SO WE CAN LIVE WITH A WEAK UNPURE SPIRIT

As we evolve into a more love based spiritual reality we will no longer have the spirit of Babylon and its greed and lust filled spirit to feed us. There will also no longer be a need for all the music, art, sports and many other things that we did to help us survive with while living in a darker reality. When we sing we impact our spirit in such a way as to make us feel better. It is the rhythm and vibration (beat) of the music that interacts with our spirit thereby creating a pleasant feeling in our body. This raises our vibration and our consciousness to a higher level. When in a darker reality many people using music to make themselves feel better will create the spirit of music.

The spirit of music and art evolved to help us feel better about ourselves when we were consumed by the pain and suffering that was a part of the spirit of Babylon. The prophecy Revelations refers to the transformation of the Spirit of Babylon and music when it says, "And the voice of harpers and musicians, and of pipers and trumpeters, shall be heard no more at all in you; and no artist of any art whatever, shall he found any more in you; and the sound of the millstone shall be heard no more in you; ..." (Rev 18:22).

When the spirit of Babylon existed in the world, mankind existed with the lack of light in our spirit. The spirit of music came into existence to give us something to make our spirits ring and our hearts sing. It was something that was needed to keep us happy when true happiness eluded our spirits and souls.

The spirit of music is what the song, "I write the Songs", sung by Barry Manilow is about. It is about the spirit of music that comes to song writers to help them write, "Songs of love and special things that make the whole world sing".

THE MARRIAGE SUPPER OF THE LAMB

The prophecy then goes on to tell the story of the "Marriage Supper of the Lamb" and "The Marriage of the Lamb". The marriage of the lamb is about learning to feed off of a new creation; the creation that will replace Babylon.

There are two things that happen simultaneously when learning to feed off this new ambient spirit created by the collective spirit of mankind. First of all it is about not feeding or feeding off of Babylon. When we stop feeding off of something that is as dark as Babylon means that it will destroy itself from within.

"And I saw an angel standing in the sun; and he cried with a loud voice, saying to all the birds that fly in mid-heaven: Come, gather yourselves to the great supper of God that you may eat the flesh of kings, and the flesh of officers, and the flesh of mighty men, and the flesh of horses, and of those who sit on them. and the flesh of all, both freemen and servants, both small and great." (Rev. 19:17 – 19:18)

The marriage supper of the lamb is also about learning to feed off the new light based creation. We do not become complete or whole until we become that which we create. Remember we create that which is a reflection of our collective spirit and soul. This final creation is going to be a little tricky to describe.

As we evolve from creating collectively from an emotion based consciousness to creating from spiritual consciousness and then from an angelic consciousness there is a different reality in who we are, how we create and what we create.

When we create (manifest) through our wants, needs, desires and cravings we created Babylon.

Then we create without these wants and need, desires and cravings we are creating from an emotional and spiritual foundation in love, mercy, acceptance, peace, wisdom, faith grace and glory etc. Creating through these foundations is not about creating what I want or need. It is about existing in a state of just being love and light and making a brighter light with every thought, word and action. In this way the new creation (the bride) of the lamb will create more love, mercy, acceptance, peace, wisdom, faith, grace, glory etc. As this new creation is being created we will learn to feed it and to feed off of it. This is the supper of the lamb.

THE DEVIL IS CHAINED FOR 1,000 YEARS AND THEN RELEASED

While letting the spirit of Babylon destroy itself and while we are creating our new reality there will be a time when the darker forces of creation (the devil) will not be able to tempt us. As we are no longer feeding or feeding off of Babylon the temptations that come with it do not exist. Temptations exist to motivate us to create from these temptations and to create more of them. When we reject these temptations we reject the darker forces of creation that come from them. So while creating this new reality that is our collective spirit we are not tempted by the devil.

After we have become one in body, spirit and soul and have created a new ambient spirit and a new reality in life we will be tempted by the devil again.

"And I saw angel come down from heaven, having the key of the abyss, and a great chain in his hand. And he laid hold of the dragon, that old serpent, which is the devil and Satan, and bound him for a thousand years, and threw him into the abyss, and shut him up, and set a seal upon him, that he should deceive the nations no more, till the thousand years should be completed; and after this he must be loosed for a little while. And I saw thrones,

and they sat upon them, and the power of judging was given to them; and I saw the souls of those who had been beheaded for the testimony of Jesus, and for the word of God; and of those who had not worshiped the beast, nor his image, and had not received his mark on their forehead, nor on their hand; and they lived and reigned with Christ a thousand years. But the rest of the dead lived not again until the 1,000 years were finished" (Rev. 20:1 – 20:5)

When the prophecy refers to the devil being bound for 1,000 years it is referring to the time it takes for the transition into this brighter light (to become one (1) in body (0), spirit (0) and soul (0)). Then when the prophecy refers to releasing the devil again for a little while it simply means that when we have effectively re-created our spirit and soul we will not fall prey to the temptations that exist. When we no longer react to or respond to these temptations we will evolve beyond the kingdom of the heavens into the kingdom of God and no longer have a need for the lessons learned from these heavens. This part of the healing process is a test to make sure that we have recreated our spirit and soul correctly. We are being judged to make sure our labor and our works have produced a reality that will not be tempted and lose its light as it did in the past. If we do not pass the test we will go back to the lesser emotions and lower vibrations of the kingdom of the heavens and start all over again until we get right.

Then our spiritual development will become an angelic reality as we continue to create what the prophecy refers to as "The New Holy City of Jerusalem". This new city will replace the old (Babylon) and become one with our resurrected self. The prophecy refers to this as the second death. The first death was when we were reborn as we learned to transform our spirit from light to dark; this second death is the resurrection from an emotional existence into a spiritual reality and then the final phase is the ascendance into the angelic reality of the kingdom of God.

Then prophecy continues saying,

"Blessed and holy is he that has part in this first resurrection; over such the second death has no power; but they shall be priests of God and of the Christ, and shall reign with him a thousand years. And when the thousand years shall have been completed, Satan shall be loosed from his prison, and shall go out to deceive the nations that are in the four corners of the earth, Gog and Magog, to bring them together to battle: the number of these is as the sand of the sea. And they went up on the breadth of the earth, and encompassed the camp of the saints, and the beloved city; and fire came down out of heaven from God, and devoured them. And the devil who deceived them was thrown into the lake of fire and brimstone, where the beast and the false prophet are; and they shall be tormented day and night from age to age. And I saw a great white throne, and him that sat upon it, from whose face the earth and the heaven fled away; and no place was found for them.

And I saw the dead, small and great, stand before the throne; and the books were opened; and another book was opened, which is the book of life; and the dead were judged out of the things that were written in the books, according to their works. And the sea gave up the dead that were in it; and death and hades gave up the dead that were in them; and they were judged, every one according to his works. And death and hades were cast into the lake of fire: this is the second death. And if any one was not found written in the book of life, he was thrown into the lake of fire." (REV. 20:6 – 20:15)

THE MARRIAGE OF THE BRIDE AND THE LAMB – THE NEW HOLY CITY OF JERUSALEM

THE 12 FOUNDATIONS OF THE SPIRIT & SOUL OF MAN AND OUR CREATIONS AT OUR HIGHEST LEVEL OF CREATION – THE STAIRWAY TO HEAVEN

The end game of our life and existence is illustrated in this final scene of the prophecy. As we evolve through the heavens; we transform the darkness that was the deep into the light and bright of the heavens and then beyond the heavens. As you learn to live in the bright light of the heavens you learn about creation and how important it is to create your light and then to maintain it. As you create a system within you, the thoughts and feelings of your spirit and soul that maintain your bright light you are integrating your body, spirit and soul. As your spirit and soul become one being in love and light you are now one step away from completing your quest. The essence of who we are grows from this final integration of your body, spirit and soul. As we become one being fully integrated in love and light we no longer need to learn the lessons that transformed us from the darkness of the deep.

This integration is more than just an individual person and the collective spirit of mankind. It is the complete integration of everyone and everything and everything inside of everything and the ambient spirit of our creations. The prophecy symbolizes this integration as the New Holy City of Jerusalem. It is about a marriage between the lamb and a bride. The lamb is our collective spirit as one being in love and light and the bride is that which we create in this highest state of mind.

There are parables about the last supper that tell the story of Jesus when he accomplished his purpose and was about to leave his friends as his spirit moved into a greater place. Just like this scene of the prophecy is one of the final chapters of the prophecy the same is true of the story of Jesus' last supper. When our purpose is complete the supper of the lamb describes the reality that is this final transformation; the completion of the purpose of creation and evolution.

The prophecy talks about a marriage supper and then the marriage of the lamb and the bride. The bride is the New Holy City of Jerusalem. The New Holy City of Jerusalem described as a city that has 12 foundations adorned in 12 Jewels and the names of the 12 apostles are on the 12 foundations. Atop the foundation is the city that has four walls and three gates on each wall. The walls are 12,000 cubits long and 12,000 cubits high and 144,000 furlongs in length. This represents the complete integration of the seven parts of the spirit with its four parts outside the body and three parts within the body; the 12 tribes of Israel with its 12,000 and 144,000 people. Inside the city walls is a river with two trees one on each side of the river. The trees have 12 fruits.

As the collective spirit and soul evolves into pure consciousness it will create 12 foundations. These 12 foundations have 3 levels and each level has 4 foundations within it:

FIRST LEVEL Physical / Emotional	SECOND LEVEL Spiritual	THIRD LEVEL Angelic
Forgive and Love	Wisdom	To be blessed
Mercy	Faith	Virtuous
Acceptance	Grace	Prophetic and Christ like
Peace	Glory	Oneness of God, Nature and Creation

The following list will show you the sequential nature through which we will evolve through creation as we create these 12 foundations in our spirit and soul, as we transcend into a being of love and light.

1) Physical/Emotional
   a. Forgive and Love
   b. Mercy
   c. Acceptance
   d. Peace
   e. Wisdom
2) Spiritual
   a. Wisdom
   b. Faith
   c. Grace
   d. Glory
3) Angelic
   a. To be blessed
   b. Virtuous
   c. Prophetic and Christ like
   d. Oneness of God, Nature and Creation

Much like we have to create a forgiving spirit we have to create all these aspects of love and light into our being.

The first level is about transforming into an emotional reality. Through the process of creation as we create a forgiving spirit, merciful spirit, an accepting spirit and, a peaceful spirit. With these four foundations built into the collective spirit of mankind we will experience another shift in our global reality.

Currently the world is transforming into an emotional reality. The transition into a spiritual realm will take just as much effort and create just as much confusion as exists in the world today. Many people today are expanding into their emotions and sensing and feeling the good and bad that exist around them. As we continue to evolve we will be able to recognize the bad as having a purpose and we will no longer think of it as bad but as an opportunity to help those in need. Helping those in need is a reality that introduces mercy into our spirit and our lives. When a person's spirit is not capable of experiencing mercy it is aggressive in nature and not very forgiving. The polar opposite of being merciful is to be aggressive and non-caring. Through a forgiving spirit the aggressive nature of mankind will naturally become merciful. To be merciful is to act on your forgiveness and love in such a way as to show mercy towards someone when they do something hurtful towards you. The first level of forgiveness is to forgive those that have hurt you in the past. As your spirit fills with light and you feel the love that flows from this level of forgiveness it is only natural to seek forgiveness from those that you have hurt in the past.

This is the second level of forgiveness and with it comes a feeling of being merciful towards others. When a person loses his or her light and the sensitivity that comes with it; it is easy to hurt others and not realize it. But after you forgive others for what they have done to you it is only natural to realize that in the past you had acted in a hurtful way towards others. With this realization and the love in your heart that now exists it is only natural to want to make amends for the hurt you caused others – this is what being merciful is all about. This will then allow you to grow into a more accepting spirit as the reality that is your life grows brighter. After you accept others for who they are and create an accepting spirit you will naturally find your peace of mind and then you will create a spirit filled with peace and your life will feel peaceful in the midst of all the chaos that might exist in it. As the light in your spirit continues to grow and the love in your heart heals your body, spirit and soul; you will naturally change the way you treat others in your day to day life. As you live to treat others better you will create a merciful spirit (a spirit filled with mercy).

After creating a merciful spirit (a spirit not capable of hurting any living thing) it is only natural to evolve into an accepting spirit. When we replace attempts to no longer judge others with a more powerful reality of creating an accepting spirit we will naturally find our peace of mind.

Currently we (mankind) are focusing our efforts to help nature; as we perceive it as having the greatest need. It is like we are being merciful towards nature but not mankind. We are not quite prepared emotionally and spiritually to help those that we see as doing evil things to one another. As we grow into greater emotions our consciousness will guide us in ways to help one another in a deeper way.

As we learn to transition into a spiritual reality we will create wisdom in our spirit (wisdom is about a consciousness that brings with it awareness and wisdom), create a faithful spirit (a spirit that functions on faith), a graceful spirit (a spirit that functions with grace) and a glorified spirit (filled with glory).

Then as we continue our evolution through creation we will be ready to make the transition into a more spiritual reality.

THE SPIRITUAL REALM

Wisdom in our spirit brings with it the consciousness required to maintain the reality we have created. It is about using the peace, acceptance and merciful nature of our spirit to do what is necessary to maintain a heightened state of awareness as to life around us. It will help us to maintain the pureness of our spirit and its rhythm and vibration. Wisdom is about being at peace with yourself and the oneness of who you are. Some may think of people that are at peace with themselves as being naïve. It is actually the complete opposite; they are aware of the hurtful actions of others and strive to maintain their light by not acting in a hurtful way towards others. They will know better than to feed the anger that manifests through the words of others. They will even be at peace when they sense and feel that others think they are weal or naïve.

To live with a spirit that has faith, not just in God but in creation, in yourself and in mankind. To truly know that all is good and what we need in life will always be there when we need it is to have a faithful spirit.

In this reality creation will test us in many ways to make sure we build this foundation effectively. Beyond the wisdom of the previous foundation we will create faith, grace and glory as we evolve into a spirit that is blessed with more than just the gift of healing. It will be as if every step a person with a blessed spirit takes will have a healing impact on others.

To create faith in your spirit and to have a spirit filled with faith is a faithful spirit. It is not just about having faith in anyone or anything but in everything you do in life. To have faith is a state of knowing that all is good. When you have faith you no longer need for anything you just know that what you need will be there when you need it. This is faith.

To create grace in your spirit – to have grace is to live with faith. A spirit filled with faith will lead to living a graceful life. To live a graceful life is to not have a care in the world. To trust so completely that all is good and the will of God's creation will guide you and provide for you is to be filled with grace.

Grace and glory are transitional in nature. They are that point in our evolution where emotions fade from the reality of our existence and are replaced with a constant feeling that is good and a consciousness that continues to flow through us throughout our day to day lives and interactions. It is no longer about creating an aspect in your life but it is about being that aspect. As a being in light grows into and experiences these higher realms of existence it is not something that is created but allowed to be within you. It is hard to put into words how it happens but as you become this transparent in your spirit and soul you just flow with every situation in your life and you let these situations flow through you.

A blessed spirit will be blessed with gifts of spirit and a natural sense of being blessed and blessing others as it creates the greatest light possible when interacting with others. When a person lives with a spirit at this level he or she will experience a heightened level of being merciful towards others. It is like living to serve other people. Today many people say that we should serve spirit but at this level of spiritual development we will feel an overwhelming desire to serve people. It is like being aware of another person's spiritual development and thriving on the opportunity to help them in the physical in such a way as to help their personal spiritual development.

THE ANGELIC REALM

The final level of our evolution is one that is angelic in nature. It is a point in evolution when we are becoming one with nature and one in nature and creation through creation. It is an incredible sensing experience. It is a reality when we are not sensing nature but sensing what nature senses. It is this twist in reality that will create a tremendous amount of confusion in a person and people collectively when are able to reach this state of being.

Then as we continue our evolution we will transcend into an angelic realm of pure consciousness. This transparent spirit will not be visible and can hardly be sensed by those of a lesser spirit and consciousness. There will be little visible difference between a virtuous or prophetic spirit as those of lesser lights will not be able to sense the difference between them. As we evolve into this transparent light we will just be at one with all in nature. We will not feel like we are one with nature we will become one with nature.

A blessed spirit will bring kindness and a sense of mercy that is unmatched. It flows through your spirit as a state of just knowing that all is good and will be good no matter what happens at any particular moment in time.

A blessed spirit will function in such a way as to bring virtue into your life.

As you learn to feed and feed off of faith, grace and glory you create a spirit that is blessed by the mere fact that it can exist in this incredible reality.

The final two higher levels of our evolution (Christ consciousness and oneness in God, nature and creation) are just beyond my ability to sense and feel. They are prophetic realities that integrate all that is into a oneness that is more than just pure consciousness. At this level, there is more to our existence than creation, evolution, mankind and nature. These last two levels will prepare us to interact with and be at peace and at one with them; whatever they may be.

The final description of the New Holy City of Jerusalem describes the city as having a river that runs though it with two trees growing on each side of the river. These trees each have 12 fruits on them. The river is the stream of consciousness that flows between the two trees that were planted earlier in the prophecy. These trees are the forgiveness and love that are needed to maintain our light and the 12 fruits are the fruits of our labor that created the 12 foundations. On one side of the stream are the emotional fruits of our labor and on the other side are the consciousness fruits of our labor. In this scene the reality of life is the pure consciousness that feeds the 12 fruits what they need in order to continue to produce more of what they are. Then as the fruits of our labor continue to create more of what they are the streams of consciousness continue to flow. This becomes the new cycle of life through which we all exist as one being of love and light.

OUR FINAL DESTINATION

Our life is about our spirit and souls existence. Life is not about me and you. Life is about all of us living together. Life is about everyone accepting everyone for who they are; not trying to change others to be like me but to accept them for who they are. Life is about re-creating the spirit of an angel.

As the collective spirit of mankind and all that we have created over time evolves into the purest of all that we can be, we will become an angel. An angelic spirit and soul is pure in intention; not pure in what I intended it to be but pure in what it is and is supposed to be.

To become one as a being of pure light is to evolve into an angel. One part of this transformation is the spirit of that which we created in the air around us throughout our existence. At the time of the prophecy it was referred to as the spirit of Babylon. Over time we will and are changing this greedy and lust filled spirit into a spirit that is more at peace within itself and with us. As we grow into a greater light and then into the greatest light possible we are re-creating the spirit that is in the air around us to be a reflection of the collective spirit of mankind. In time the evolution of mankind will grow into one being of pure love and light that will create nothing more than its own pureness.

Becoming one with all that we created is not the same as integrating everything into our being.

The kingdom of the heavens is where we learn about how to create and how our body, spirit and soul work together to create the spirit of whom we are and now the spirit we create impacts our day to day lives.

When we are ready to grow beyond the kingdom of the heavens we are ready to just be. This means that we are not trying to create anything. We just exist as one with everything; this was the original state that Adam was supposed to exist in. To just be, not is to consciously create, but to become a part of creation. To not consciously create will leave the past creations behind. As we leave them behind they will not be fed by any emotions or consciousness and will just fade away and no longer exist.

To have a virtuous reality in your life is to live with the blessings of a blessed spirit. It is to walk the talk of being, righteous, caring, loving and compassionate. To be virtuous is more than just knowing that all is good but to be good. It is to walk the talk of being of the highest and the best. Many can talk about the highest best but few if any today can actually be a being that is of the best. It is not just about saying and doing kind things it is about being a kind person. To be kind is to live to care and feel deeply for more than just other people but for all life. This high moral standard is a standard of pureness that few today can even fathom or attempt to imagine. We can all think we know what a high moral standard is but to achieve this level of pureness cannot even be imagined by most people in today's society and world. The pureness of this white light is very hard to describe but to feel the weightlessness of being virtuous is truly to feel the light of an angel. To be virtuous is to transcend the physical reality as you become more than just human but to reach for the skies of a realm of feeling and knowing that is angelic in nature, angelic in creation. To just be aware of all that is through simple actions of caring and being compassionate is to transcend into the angelic realms of the highest and best possible reality in life. To say these words and to realize the reality of living in this pureness are two very different things in today's society; many talk about it but few if any can actually understand it or achieve it.

At lower levels of spiritual evolution we become one in body, spirit and soul at this highest level of evolution we become one with nature and creation. At lower levels of living in the light the body, spirit and soul integrate into one being of love and light. To transcend from this state of being in love and light to pure consciousness is to transcend the light and become one with nature and creation. To be one in body spirit and soul is to act in a synchronized manner with your body, spirit and soul. To transcend into a state of oneness with nature and creation is to transcend beyond the need to be in life and to just be with everything that is inside of everything. Everything inside of everything is all that is nature and creation. To be virtuous is the key to this transcendental reality of life and existence.

In time we will all evolve into this highest light of pure love and compassion. Throughout this book we have discussed the personal spirit, collective spirit of mankind and the ambient spirit of mankind. When we evolve collectively into this higher light we are integrating these three realities of our spiritual existence into one being which is the end game for the reality of creation that is body, spirit and soul. This end game is the final stage of the process that re-creates an angel. This is why the prophecy used seven angels in seven churches and seven angels with trumpets and holding cups to represent the collective spirit of mankind.

The prophecy "The Revelation of Christ" refers to this reality of creation when it says,

"And he measured the wall of it, a hundred and forty-four cubits, the measure of a man, that is, of an angel." (Rev. 21:17)

CHAPTER 6

MESSAGES FROM THE PROPHECY

Creation and evolution

Time and the end of times

The prodigal son

The four horsemen

Forgiveness

    Living with love and light & living a purposeful life

Collectively forgiving the sins of the past

How to live so you can continue to evolve

    Grow beyond the collective spirit of mankind

Accept that you are doing and always have done the best you can with what you have; with who you are

Think and feel before you speak or act

What do you fill your cups with?

What happens when you die?

Our current evolution

    Learning to love

Human nature

A dream, vison or prophecy comes to a person as the answer to a deep seeded question or need. When we have a deep need to know something the spirit of the need to know will present the answer to us in a dream. One of the most famous examples of this is when the vision the Egyptian pharaoh had about seven camels. He dreamed that seven healthy camels were approaching a pond or lake and in the second scene he saw seven unhealthy camels walking away from the pond or lake. The pharaoh had many spiritual people that would normally interpret these dreams for him; but they would not tell him what this one meant. He made an example of several by killing them but the others would not tell him what the dream meant. That is when he found the slave Joseph to interpret it for him. This dream came to the pharaoh because he wanted to know something. It is all that truly mattered to him. When the dream came to him he knew he had to know the answer and was going to do whatever it took to find the answer. His deep seeded need is seen in the result of his actions. What he wanted to know was how to control and rule over the entire Middle East. The dream meant that seven years of famine and drought were coming to the Middle East. With that dream he implanted a plan take all the money, land and homes of all the people affected by the drought that was coming. He could have warned everyone that the drought was coming and they could have learned to survive together but that was not what was truly in his heart. But at that time the spirit of man was not capable of working together cooperatively. Hopefully we can create a more positive reality in our future.

The prophecy, "The Revelation of Christ" came to ST John in a similar manner. ST John had a deep seeded desire to know what was going to happen to mankind. He was concerned about the lessons that Jesus was teaching and if mankind would ever learn from him. I would imagine this seemed like a daunting reality at that time in our history. This vision came to ST John many years (maybe 50 years) after Jesus died. He knew Jesus' message was about saving the spirit of man but he had to have doubts about how effective it would be. After Jesus died it was ST Paul's teachings that became the prominent teachings that people would follow. The leaders of the Israelites encouraged people to listen to him and ST Paul was not teaching what Jesus taught. He did not even speak in parables or explain the message of the parables. He was teaching what he believed was the truth. His teachings were good but not what Jesus was teaching. I would imagine that ST John was very concerned about Jesus' message and what would happen to mankind. This is why the prophecy came to him.

This prophecy does not predict future events. It explains creation and how creation works through evolution. It explains the evolution of mankind over time. It has messages for all of mankind at any point in time. At any point in time it tells us what we need to know when we need to know it. This is how creation works. Creation will tell us what we need to know when we need to know it; therefore the prophecy should do the same. What the prophecy would tell mankind today is explained in this last chapter of this book.

The prophecy has many messages both specific to an individual reader and to the world collectively. It has messages that are specific to a generation at a point in time and messages that are specific to creation and how it works. Below are just a few that are pertinent to mankind today. I would encourage everyone to read the prophecy and this book to learn what it might tell you about your life.

CREATION AND EVOLUTION

Creation and evolution are the first realties of creation.

A person creates all day long every day. We create the spirit of who we are at every moment in time; at every moment in creation. It is through our thoughts, words and actions that creation is made possible.

Creation is not about manifesting what I want or what you want in life.
Creation is not about making the world what you want it to be.
Creation is not about being making you into the person you want to be; therefore trying to make yourself something that you are not. Many people believe they should believe they are something and then they will change. While it is possible to assert your will on to your-self in such a way as to modify your personal spirit so it will make you feel better. This is not going to change your personal spirit and then make your life better. This will only manifest a vibration in your spirit that will make you think that you have changed. No substantive change comes from this.

Creation is about how we evolve throughout our lives.
Creation is about living life and just being who you are; who we are, and then letting creation (God) do the rest.
The most important thing to learn from this book is that a person creates individually and we create collectively.

Evolution is the expansion of mankind collectively, as we evolve into greater emotions and a higher consciousness.
It is through the processes of creation and forces of creation that interact on each and every one of us individually and collectively that evolution happens. We are evolving and getting stronger in spirit every day because that is simply how it works, how it is supposed to be. How fast we evolve is a function of how seriously we take things like seeking forgiveness and finding deep emotional responses to events in our lives. We evolve faster and with greater strength in our collective spirit when we are sincere in how we express ourselves. Do we mean what we say or do we strive to tell people what they want to hear? We have to be sincere and we will

then thrive in our lives. We will grow even stronger when we stop trying to not judge others and instead accept others for who they are.

TIME AND THE END OF TIMES

A time in creation is the time needed for an intention or purpose to be completed. For example the end of a time is when Adam became a complete being; when the lord God breathed life into him and created a complete being. This is a time that allowed the spirit and soul to become a complete being. This marked the end of a time in creation.

When Adam and Eve became a broken spirit and were clothed in skin was the end of another time. This end of a time marked two realities in creation; the first was the evolution of mankind in the physical sense and the second was the evolution of the spirit and soul on its journey.

The next time, evolved from the time when the human body, spirit and soul became a reality in time and when Moses demonstrated unconditional love for the Israelites. This unconditional love released the seals on the book of knowledge of love and light. Releasing these seals allowed creation to exist as a reality in our lives but creating in love and light did not exist after Moses lost his love for them 40 years later.

The next time in creation was supposed to be when the Israelites evolved into a healthier collective spirit. But it did not work and the power of creation spread throughout all of mankind. This led to the collective spirit of mankind evolving into the darker reality of an unhealthy spirit. Mankind evolved into it darkest reality when Jesus came and planted the seeds of forgiveness and love in the collective spirit of mankind.

Currently we are living and creating at a point in time that will mark the end of the time that Jesus was talking about in his parables. Through the efforts of many generations we have now allowed the seeds of forgiveness and love to grow as we have begun to generate forgiveness and love (love of God, Nature and Creation) in the collective spirit of mankind. This marks the end of one time and the beginning of another.

The prophecy refers to a time and times and a half a time until we have completed our quest to become whole again. A time contains a significant spiritual event like Moses demonstrating unconditional love for the Israelites and mankind's experiences that result from the impact of this spiritual reality. The Catholic Churches Bible refers explains one time in our history in two parts referred to as "Exodus" and "The Old Testament". "Exodus" is when Moses demonstrated unconditional love thereby releasing the seals that sealed our fate in a darker reality and "The Old Testament" chronicles the events that occurred as the Israelites created though the power of creation for the first time. The phrase time and times and a half a time refers to the commitment that is needed to continue these processes of creation. Nature and creation are here for us for as long as we need them.

THE PRODIGAL SON

At some point in time over the last 2,000 years mankind reached its prodigal son moment and has committed to our quest to find our light. This means it has become human nature to resolve the issues in our lives. In the last 100 years psychiatrists, psychologists and counselors have worked to gain a better understanding of the brain, mind and how they work. Many people are striving to learn more about how to live a holistic lifestyle. Hopefully the information in this book will help someone that is one their quest to learn more about how the mind, body, spirit and soul work together to shape our lives.

Today many people are searching for different ways to find love and light in their lives. In the end whatever method you use to deal with your issues in life it will involve forgiveness.

Everyone that has been on their journey in life will have a moment in time, a moment in their life, when they will realize they are not as good as they think they are; they will accept the truth that their spirit is un-pure and then begin their quest. Without the realization that we are in a bad place spiritually we will never have the strength needed to commit to your quest to find our light. This prodigal son moment will mark a time in our lives when we will begin our quest to create a light-based spirit. It is not until this moment that they will begin this quest. When you do begin this quest you will realize that there is a big difference between not feeling anger and feeling the love that comes from the light side of the heavens. Then after forgiveness and love enter your life you will grow into higher levels of light in your spirit as you learn to create the brighter lights of mercy, acceptance, peace, faith and more.

Please remember this is a natural occurrence in everyone's life. It is human nature to dis-evolve and then to evolve.

THE FOUR HORSEMEN

The seven seals that seal a book contain four riders on horses. It is imperative that everyone in this world constantly strive to tame these horses from within you. We all have issues in our lives. Try not to deny this reality of life. This world existed for thousands of years and throughout those years created a lot of bad stuff in our collective spirit and in the air around us. Life time after life time and generation after generation we have been returning so we can cleanse all of it from us. We all have things that we have to do so we can evolve from dark to light or from light to bright or into pure consciousness. It is not important to know where each and every one of us is as it relates to our consciousness. What is important is that we always strive to do better. Do not get complacent and think or believe that you are done – it is a journey and a quest – do the best you can with what you have and who you are. Creation is perfect and will take care of you as you take care of you.

FORGIVENESS

     a. Individually
     b. Collectively – Islam & Israel

LIVING WITH LOVE AND LIGHT & LIVING A PURPOSEFUL LIFE

Forgiveness is more than just saying I forgive you or asking someone to forgive you. It is about creating a forgiving spirit.

In order to create a forgiving spirit you have to forgive or ask for forgiveness with so much intensity that at the moment of forgiveness you are fully committed to it. It is the intensity you commit to it that creates the spirit of forgiveness within your spirit and around you. When you are fully committed to forgiving someone, you will naturally commit the most positive emotions that you are capable of bringing through you to the act of forgiveness. When you do this you will create an amount of forgiveness that is equal to the amount of love you put into the act of forgiveness. The amount of forgiveness you are capable of creating is a function of the amount of love you are capable of using. Then you will receive that much forgiveness in your spirit. As your spirit becomes more forgiving it will become stronger. This greater strength will allow you to use a greater amount of love when you forgive someone in the future. It is this process of re-creating your spirit that will add strength to you and your spirit as you create a forgiving spirit. Then you have to learn to live with a love-based spirit. This is what all have to do to create a cup (spirit) that is strong enough to hold light.

Living with a love-based spirit will bring a greater sincerity to your day to day life; to your day to day interactions with others. With sincerity in your day to day life you will co-create an even greater (brighter) spirit through your relationships with others. Sincerity will naturally evolve into a greater purpose in your life. As you live with purpose your life will become more purposeful. A purposeful life will evolve into a life filled with purpose. A life filled with purpose will create a powerful reality in your life as your purpose guides you through your day to day interactions. This is the process we all need to use to fill our cups (spirit) with the bright light of your purpose.

COLLECTIVELY FORGIVING THE SINS OF THE PAST

The most important and most powerful message of the prophecy relates to creating forgiveness in the collective spirit of two groups of people – Islam and Israel. Only after both Islam and Israel learn to forgive one another and create a forgiving spirit within and between their nations will the world evolve into all that it can be.

The prophecy uses these two groups as an example of the need to create forgiveness at a collective level. But the need is much greater than just these two groups. We all know the reason we judge others or are prejudiced against them is because of a basic fear related to the other person or group of people. Throughout many centuries people have acted on their fear of others in such a way as to create little islands of beliefs. For a long time people felt comfortable with a belief that they are right about something in order to gain greater comfort by also making themselves different from others they deemed or judged as wrong. It was fear that makes people not want to be like someone else so they gather together with others that have a similar belief and can feel stronger by being a part of the collective they associate with. Whether it is a religious collective or by nationality or by career or any of a number of other ways that the collective spirit of mankind has divided itself in today's society. It is like people were swimming in a sea of their own fear of others and their fears allowed them to perceive sharks were in the water with them. Through these fears they gathered together as a larger group in order to feel safer and to create a belief that they are better than the others they feared. As they created these beliefs that made them feel safe they created an island that is their belief. Then the sharks that are their fears became another island. Then others became afraid of the larger groups and further divided themselves into more divisive groups. Now as the groups became smaller and the fears became greater more islands were created. Now people are trying to make it so their islands are farther away from the other islands. They make their islands farther apart by finding ways to disagree with the beliefs of others.

Today there are a lot of dolphins that swim in between these islands. Some people might call them angels. They are here to help us to find ways to agree on these truths not continue to create divisions between us but to integrate and unite us as one. But only we can take those first steps back into the water and learn to trust one another again. We have to wade into these waters that led us to fear one another. We do this by searching for ways to agree with one another instead of taking the easy way and following the lead of others that believe they are right and everyone should listen to them tell us how they are going to save our souls. Only I can save my soul and only you can save yours and no can tell us what we have to do to walk our path.

So go ahead take the lead and start to walk your path and to swim in the pool of everyone else's fears. You might just find that there is nothing to be afraid; your soul will be just as secure or insecure no matter who you listen too. Seek out those that will encourage you to live without fear and to find your way not to follow them on their path. Following someone else's path will only allow you to see what they needed to do to find their light. Most likely it is not your path though.

HOW TO LIVE SO YOU CAN CONTINUE TO EVOLVE

GROW BEYOND THE COLLECTIVE SPIRIT OF MANKIND

It is ok to do what everyone else does so you can feel accepted by others.

But, it you really want to feel great without the need to be accepted you have to go outside of this box of feelings. You can feel great just because you can. It is not about being a loner.

It is about accepting you for who you are and then doing what you know is the right thing to do. Then to no longer need to be accepted by others will lead to a greater sincerity in what you say, think and do.

You know what the right the right thing to do is; so just do it. Do what you feel and know is the right thing to do. Do not be afraid that others will try to mock you or make you feel uncomfortable for doing what you know is right. They will do this and when you just walk away from their envy, anger and resentment you will feel good about your-self. Your spirit will then become stronger. You have to set this as a standard for yourself and commit to it and then you will feel good about just being you. This is what living with a spirit that is pure is all about. The lesser light personal spirits and darker spirits are still waiting for others to tell them how good they are. But they will never truly feel great about themselves until they learn to be righteous and do the right thing just because it is the right thing to do.

ACCEPT THAT YOU ARE DOING AND ALWAYS HAVE DONE THE BEST YOU CAN WITH WHAT YOU HAVE; WITH WHO YOU ARE

Accept one simple reality or fact of truth. Accept that what you do today is the best you can with what you have. Accept that the truth is that you will evolve; you will grow into a greater spirit and higher consciousness. Accept that the truth is that with a higher consciousness you will learn to change everything about you and those you associate with throughout your life. Accepting this is a very important reality of creating an accepting spirit.

To live, love and laugh is to raise your spirit to the highest level you can with the limits that might exist within your spirit. You will always receive the best possible thoughts when you raise your spirit in this way. Then use the thoughts that come to you. Learn to listen to these thoughts and then learn to apply them in your life. Always accept thoughts that come from happiness, love and compassion. They will always guide you in a better way than anger-based thoughts. Follow these thoughts that come from a positive spirit even if you think you might be wrong or making a mistake.

While writing this book I was not concerned about being right or wrong I just accepted what came to me and the typed it. When I was done I read what I wrote and it was perfect. Before these truths could flow through my consciousness, I had to accept the fact that whatever I was writing could be wrong. If I only wanted to write what others would accept I would have received completely different information. But my intention to learn what the prophecy was about grew into a purpose to learn the truths within it. As my purpose grew stronger from within me these truths began to make sense and I started typing. I typed for 24 hours a day, 7 days a week until it was completed 9 months later. Then I read it and it made sense. This is how blind faith grew in my spirit. I not only had faith but acted on it as I typed with no concern as to what I was going to end up with. Now four years later my life has changes and I am confident I am on the right path in my life as I continue on my quest.

THINK AND FEEL BEFORE YOU SPEAK OR ACT

If you want to create the best possible life for yourself and relationships for yourself and others the first thing you have to learn to do is to sense and feel. Learn to know what you are feeling when you say or do something. Then learn to sense and feel before you speak. When you are comfortable that you can control your actions learn to control the feelings you put into your words and actions. When you sense or feel that you are stressed, angry or even upset about something – do not act on these feelings. All you have to do is wait until these feelings subside and then think about what you want to say or do. With a fresh spirit you may say or do the same thing you would have done when stressed or angry but the spirit of your words will be different.

WHAT DO YOU FILL YOUR CUPS WITH

One way the prophecy describes our individual and collective spirits is as cups that can be filled or emptied. When our spirit was filled with plagues our cups were filled with a personal spirit that was not pure. As we learned to forgive and love we cleansed our personal spirits and were able to create from a love based reality. This is what the Prophecy refers to as Babylon being divided into three parts. We are currently creating the collective spirit of mankind to exist in both a light and dark reality. We are not yet in the bright light but will get there soon.

It is important to understand that we have to create a way of life that will allow us to live in both a competitive reality and in a reality that allows us to thrive on creating a better world. Both light and dark have to exist together. Then as some people grow into the bright light of the heavens we will have to create physical systems that will allow people to live with their passion for life. As we create these three physical realities we will create the ambient spirit of learning to live in the light and the ambient spirit of living in the bright light of these heavens. After these three realities exist it is only a matter of time until everyone evolves into the bright light or unconditional love and this is how we create, "The Fall of Babylon".

It is absolutely imperative that governments all around world create a way of life that will facilitate the growth of their societies in such a way as to allow people with intense anger and love and compassion to live together. Some people will be comfortable striving to survive while others will want to thrive in their life. We need to view both life styles as equal. Those in that live in society with intense anger need to co-exist with those that are learning to leave their anger in the past. Those that simply want to live with a deep rooted passion for life not just a passion for money and things will create a better way of life for all. The challenge is that people that want to express their anger and live to have things need their things and need to over consume in order to survive. It will be a great challenge for leaders of future generations as they strive to create a world that is acceptable to all; especially to those that still judge others and find it difficult to accept anything that anyone does. There are political groups today that have built their foundation on disagreeing. They will refuse to accept whatever their leaders do. It is this in ability to "accept" that drives this wedge between its members.

This is happening and will continue to happen into future generations. The good news is that future generations of children and adults will have a greater spirit and a higher consciousness and the solutions will come to them naturally. They just have to be willing to make a mistake as they try something different. Just like politicians today that make a difference and create changes in society, they will be persecuted by those that have weaker spirits. Be strong in who you are and just do what you know is the right thing to do and all will be good.

WHAT HAPPENS WHEN YOU DIE

Now that you have read this book you should have an in depth understanding of who you are in body, spirit and soul. When your spirit and soul leave your body you are the memories, feelings and emotions that you lived with at the end of your physical life. The experiences you had in your life no matter how difficult they were for you did shape you into the person that you are. You have re-created yourself. You have made you a better you. Who you are in spirit is the result of how you reacted to various situations throughout your life. You take the results of the fruits of your labor with you into the afterlife. Your labor and your works are the process that reshapes you; your spirit and soul.

OUR CURRENT EVOLUTION - LEARNING TO LOVE

Many people today are, for the first time, feeling love again. For thousands of years the closest we came to feeling love was to not feel anger, hatred or rage, ire, distain or wrath. It feels so good to be able to choose to have this level of love instead of an anger based emotion that we think we have achieved a great success. While we have achieved a great success it really is only a small step in the right direction. There is a much greater love that awaits those of future generations. We need to learn collectively right now to <u>share</u> the love we feel and to accept even greater emotions into our lives. The faster we learn to live with this light and love, mercy, acceptance, peace, wisdom and faith the better off we are all going to be. It is not just about saying that I have faith and then expecting God to take of everything for me. It is about truly believing that all is good and whatever your problems are will be dealt with in time. Do not just leave it up to your God to create love in your life, go out and do it yourself. Deal with the sadness in your life, forgive those that wish you harm or create harmful environments in your, home, neighborhood or at work. Forgiving and loving those that wish you harm is the greatest tool in your tool box. It totally disarms those that wish you harm. They cannot create more of who they are when you reject the spirit of their thoughts, words and actions. You reject them by forgiving them. Next you have to stop trying to not judge others. Not being judgmental is OK but to create an accepting spirit is light years better. If you are struggling to not judge others then try to accept them for who they area and the judgment will go away. Peace of mind will naturally follow acceptance then wisdom will bring thoughts into your life you will need to maintain this brighter level of spiritual existence.

This was a message from God; from your collective spirit that is struggling to create a brighter light from within it.

HUMAN NATURE

As you learned from reading this book, human nature is an accepted way of life. Human nature exists when three or more generations in a row accept the spirit of their behaviors as the only possible way to live. The story of the four horsemen, seven seals and the great city of Babylon describe human nature and how it evolved throughout time. For more than 3,000 years we have learned to rely on trade for our survival. Today, younger generations are breaking the mold that is the foundation of this belief. They are not interested in carrying on this destructive reality. The older generations fear for the future and the future of this younger generation. Many people of the older generations cannot see a future without these systems that are based on hard work and taking pride in what you do. As the younger generations search for a better way, they will find it. This is how Babylon is dividing herself before your eyes.

The world will need to develop a way of life that will accommodate:

1) The more traditional way of life that allows people to work and have pride in what they do.
2) A way of life that will allow those that do not want the destructive, competitive pride filled way of life to infect their peace of mind.
3) There will always be a way of life that that is always striving to make things better than the way they are.

This is going to change the nature of the generation gap. As generations of children grow into adults they will have vastly more love, light, acceptance, peace of mind and consciousness than the previous generations. With this greater light in their collective spirit and higher consciousness they will find ways to allow a full range of realities to evolve simultaneously in the world. It is interesting how this world can accommodate everyone if we just let it. After all it is only natural to do so; it is only natural to live and let live.

THE GRAND FINALE

When the people that are mankind learn to agree instead of disagree with one another we will have re-created our-selves and found our perfect light. Truth lies in learning from one another. When we evolve beyond disagreeing and learn to agree we will find greater truths in life. To know what is right or best and for everyone to know the same thing is when we all share the same consciousness. This will mark the end of our need to live in a world and have a physical life. After we complete our quest and exist in pure consciousness, a state of being will exist in the Son of Man; in the oneness that is us.

THE MORAL OF THE PROPHECY

The moral of the story is that we are a part of a much larger reality – the collective spirit of mankind. Our lives are about having an impact on our collective spirit. As we live to make our life better we make it better. We do have an impact on everyone; the brighter the light of our spirit the greater our impact on others.

Knowing that the reality of life hinges on that moment in time when we realize that our spirit is un-pure and sleeping with the pigs can be a bit disconcerting; as if we have no control over re-creating our spirit. I found this reality to be a bit of a relief. The key to living in this world and enjoying our lives while at the same time doing what is best for all of mankind is simply to <u>live</u>, <u>love</u> and <u>laugh</u>; and then do good.

When you have learned to forgive and live you simply add another step by learning to listen to your inner voice and then learn by doing.
When I say live I mean to really live and make the best of every moment in your life. This will create a higher vibration in your spirit.
When I say love I mean to put as much positive emotion into everything you say, think and do. This will create a higher vibration in everything you create especially your personal spirit.
Laughter helps us all enjoy the moments we have together as we co-create a better world.

To listen to your inner voice and to turn on the good and turn off the bad can be a challenge for some but the more you practice doing good, the better it will be for you and your spirit. When your inner voice only encourages you to do good and your conscience no longer challenges you to not do hurtful things to others, you know that you are on the right track. Now all you have to do is to use what you know. As you just know the right thing to do in various situations and then do it with a much love as you can, you are living your life with purpose. Your soul's consciousness will now continue to bring more things into your life so you can accomplish your purpose, as you learn to live, love and laugh at an even higher level you can continue to learn to remake your life over and over again.

In the end this healing process is all about relationships. It is about:

1) Your relationship with God, Nature and Creation.
2) Your relationship with yourself.
3) Your relationship with others especially family and close and friends.
4) Your relationship with those that wish you harm.

Peace and Love

Phoenix